Three Snapshots of Reality

Three Snapshots of Reality

Don E. Stevens

with Wayne Smith

COMPANION BOOKS
PUBLISHERS

Three Snapshots of Reality
By Don E. Stevens with Wayne Smith

Published by Companion Books

First Printing: February 25, 2014.
ISBN: 978-0-9565530-0-3

Printed by LightningSource
An Ingram Content Company
1246 Heil Quaker Blvd.
La Vergne, TN 37086 USA

Cover and book design by Ralph Schmid
www.ralphschmid.com

Front cover photos by Laurent Weichberger
and chapter "Don Stevens: A Short Biography"
copyright © 2014 by L. Weichberger, and used by permission.

Photo of Don E. Stevens on the back cover by Hasan Selisik,
who said "Don was our guide (or only Hasan's) to Beloved Baba.
Taken during a two day gathering at Don's apartment in Cagnes sur Mer,
France in 1979." Copyright © 2014 Hasan Selisik, and used by permission.

Photo of Avatar Meher Baba facing "Meher Baba: A Short Biography," copyright (c)
2014 by Martin Cook. Used by permisson.

All quotes from Meher Baba in referenced literature are copyright (c) 2014 Avatar
Meher Baba Perpetual Public Charitable Trust unless otherwise noted:

Avatar Meher Baba Trust,
King's Road, Post Bag 31, Ahmednagar MS, 414 001, India
(www.ambppct.org)

❦

Contents

Meher Baba: A Short Biography   7

Don Stevens: A Short Biography   11

Introduction   38

Three Snapshots of Reality   44

Photo Section   62

Honesty   75

Meher Baba and Finances   82

Ivy O. Duce and Sufism Reoriented   95

The Body and Diet   102

Head and Heart   105

Meher Baba's Manifestation   116

Bhau Kalchuri   125

Glossary   130

Acknowledgments   132

Avatar Meher Baba portrait by photographer: Kinye Imai (London, 1931), courtesy of Martin Cook.

Meher Baba: A Short Biography

By Wayne Smith

Not all who open this book will be familiar with the name Meher Baba. He was born in 1894 in the Indian city of Pune and raised in the Zoroastrian community as Merwan Sheriar Irani. A fairly normal childhood ensued, until a series of encounters with local spiritual masters led him to experience the reality of his own spiritual status. This unveiling eventually found Merwan revered by many of his close friends and extended family as a Perfect Master, and by the early 1920s he was commonly referred to as Meher Baba — *the Compassionate Father*. In 1954 he let it be known that he was in fact the Avatar, the one expected by the many, but in his lifetime known only by a few.

The term Avatar is another word you might also encounter for the first time here. It is an ancient Hindu term — literally "incarnation"— a concept which refers specifically to the pulling down of transcendent God into a visible, tangible form. This manifestation is usually experienced by humanity as being that of another human being: what has been referred to in other traditions as the "Rasool," or "Christ," or the "Messiah." But, as Meher Baba explains, this most magical and exalted of all spiritual transformations isn't just restricted to the human form, for whenever God is brought down into Creation, like crystal veined through rock or sunlight that cuts through dust, "… God mingles with mankind as man and with the world of ants as an ant, etc. But the man of the world cannot perceive this and hence simply says that God has become man and remains satisfied with this understanding in his own world of mankind."

This concept of the Avatar perfectly captures for me the very essence of who Meher Baba was and really is. For where do you start in the attempt to describe the indescribable, in the wish to place the ineffable within words — it's like trying to pour a shoreless ocean into a cup, or folding an infinite blue sky away inside your pocket. As such, it is one of my favorite notions in all the spirituality that I have so far encountered, especially as this incarnating of God doesn't just happen the once, but occurs periodically "... whenever there is too much evil in the world," as Krishna explained to Arjuna all those years ago. It is a truth, I feel, that holds the most true of all truths. And for many of us today Meher Baba, as the Avatar of this age, simply is who he says he is.

Don Stevens and Laurent Weichberger in California, October 22, 2010.
Photo by Mahmoud Ajang.

Don Stevens: A Short Biography

My Beautiful Big Bear and an Elder Brother in Avatar Meher Baba's Love
January 14, 1919 – Imlay, Nevada until April 26, 2011 – London, England.

By Laurent Weichberger
Half Moon Bay, California
July 2013

I am sitting in Don's London apartment at 228 Hammersmith
Grove, having been here all week for work. I asked if I could stay
here, instead of a fancy hotel — I wasn't sure why, I just knew I
wanted to be here. When I arrived it was stark and Spartan as it was
being prepared for sale. All the Baba photos had been taken down
and put in storage in the Meher Baba Association, which occupies
the basement flat below. Don's room was sparse, no beds, no books,
just old linens, and a lone sweater on a hanger in his closet, with
a few ties on a tie rack. Sigh. In the living room all that remained
were the couch and two chairs we had chosen together at Ikea with
Claude many years before, and a dining room table and six chairs.
Somehow the six chairs helped me realize that Don is gone. We used
to sit with Don around that table during spiritual gatherings with
food and wine, and as anyone who has participated remembers,
the conversations during those meals could be deeper and more
meaningful than the planned topic for the Baba meeting. Real
community — real spiritual companionship.

Lol Benbow had come to fetch me at the airport and give me
keys to the flat, and together we went about beautifying it once
again. We got Baba (and Mehera) back up on the walls, and tidied
up. This morning, sitting in the backyard, with the two years plus of
overgrown garden, damp feet on wet flagstone I realized how much I
miss Don. For those who never met him and are just learning about
Don's life and work with and for Meher Baba, all I can say here is

that he was the embodiment of friendship and lovingkindness. He wouldn't want me to leave it there, because he had a keen intellect and would use that sharp mind of his in direct service of his heart and his spiritual life. Meher Baba said, "Don has an almost perfect balance of mind and heart," indicating that such a balance was vital spiritually.

I once asked Don directly, how does one do this work of "balancing the mind and the heart?" And in his usual matter of fact style he said, "Okay, well, when you have a thought about something, before you do it, ask yourself — how does my heart feel about that? And if you are feelings something deeply, before you react and start down a path, say — what do I think about that, really?" In this simple manner, he suggested, we could get both sides involved, and have a more balanced approach to just about everything in life. Another time we compared our approach to Meher Baba, and the spiritual life (this was shortly after I moved to England to work on his biography), and I asked him about his spiritual outlook with Baba. After hearing my way, he said, "... I try to bring as much love as I can to every situation, every meeting, every transaction in life." He was a Sufi in the real sense of the word, and he never ever left Sufism. As he told me, when we discussed that subject, "Once a Sufi always a Sufi."

I remember how I first met Don. We had been working on a couple of small writing projects, and had only sent emails back and forth. He requested an article from me about a subject of importance to him ({not sure parentheses are really needed, could cut them}for publication in the newsletter *Neti Neti*), and we had come to the point where there was just too much to discuss by email. He was about to go to the Meher Spiritual Center to meet with a group of Baba lovers with whom he was writing his newest book, *Meher Baba's Gift of Intuition*. He said all the chapters had been assigned already, but if I wanted to, he would invite me to "audit" the meetings, wherein they would write, and share their chapters, and move the book project along. I said yes.

That summer of 2002, I drove with my small family to Myrtle Beach, and before I knew it I was speaking to Don in the meeting hall of the Center, just before his talk about *God Speaks* to those gathered. He was standing with Joan Agin, and myself, and said to me, "Excuse me — " and then turned to Joan and asked, "Do you know where I can find Laurent Weichberger?" Joan and I laughed, and she replied, "This is Laurent!" Then Don also laughed.

After Don's Baba talk, he explained that we had to meet off-Center for the book project, as there were no "closed group" meetings allowed on the Center. So we had our sessions for the next days over at local Baba lover homes in the community. After each day of long meetings, where each of the Baba authors shared their chapters and requested feedback from Don and group, Don invited me back to his cabin to share more with him personally. Don was staying with Claude Longuet, and we three spent hours sharing about Baba, and intuition, usually with Claude preparing dinner in the kitchen. I had been taking notes all day while auditing the day's meetings, and I was incredibly interested in this whole process.

Each evening Don asked me a lot of questions regarding the day long work sessions we had just been through with the authors, about the upcoming intuition book.

I asked if he wanted me to be honest, and he said he did. So I took out my notes, and we went over them. He seemed to love my honesty, and the chance to discuss all of it deeply.

This book was published as *Meher Baba's Gift of Intuition* (London: Companion Books, 2006).

It was like finally meeting a Baba lover who spoke exactly the same language as me, and he was surrounded by spiritual companions of such variety and mystical depth that I just knew this was my "tribe." This went on for three days, and on the fourth day Don announced that Jack Small and I would write a chapter for the book. He never asked me, he just told us all. I was thrilled.

❧

Don Stevens was born on January 14, 1919, in Imlay, Nevada, the youngest of three brothers: Earl (oldest), then Wilfred, and finally came Don. About this early time in his life, Don wrote a story called simply, "Mustang," which our companion Kathy Harris sent me recently:

My memories of the wild mustang in Nevada and my first horseback ride date no doubt to the age of being about three years old, as I was five when we moved to California. So we were still in the little town of Imlay, population 98 persons. We had a small house on the edge of the village with a kitchen garden and two or three small, fenced-in chicken runs. One of these was used only when Mom was raising a new spring batch of baby chicks, and before she bought them each year I could remember my brothers getting permission to go into the sandhills below the Sierra Nevada Mountains to lasso a wild mustang, which they would bring home and put into the unused chicken run. Gradually they would tame the mustang and then ride it and finally dispose of it in a manner I was never told about.

In the spring I saw all the preparations for getting the mustang, and shortly thereafter saw them leading a fine-looking animal into the unused yard. Some days later it became the custom to ride the horse during the afternoon and pen it just before our early family dinner. Then studies by my brothers, and early lights out and to bed.

I had the right after dinner to go out and join [my best friends] Cookie and Jackie for a short play period. Thus on the evening in question, I excused myself from [the] table and went out the back door leading through the back garden and the chicken runs. As I passed the one inhabited by the mustang, he saw me and came towards the fence. He snuffled and looked positively friendly and not wild at all, so I talked to him and he came closer. Spontaneously and with no fixed plan, I coaxed him close to the fence where there was a solid board holding up the wiring. All this was arranged so I could get to it and have a way to pet the horse. This was accomplished easily, and then one thing led to another.

First thing I knew I was at the side of the horse and slightly above him on the board holding the fence wiring. I put my hand on the neck of the horse. He looked at me. I put one leg tentatively over his back and down his far side. He looked at me again. I looked at him. There was no sign of anything being forbidden, so I lowered myself onto him, and he turned his head to look at me. We did a few steps of trials and nothing happened. I nudged him to the gate for the chicken run.

He looked back at me as if to question what I wanted to do. I nodded my head and lifted the wire hoop up from the movable end of the primitive gate frame and swung the gate out. My horse knew what an open gate was and calmly walked through it and into the little alley that passed at the end of our modest plot of land.

As if by common consent we went to the first branching from the alley towards the sand hills only yards away, and calmly we continued into the terrain where I knew every dune and bit of sage brush in the entire border to the little village. It was rapidly becoming dark, my normal warning that my playtime with Cookie and Jackie should terminate before mother called out to me to come home. But the stars were out to lighten the way for my companion and me, so we wandered on without the slightest reason or plan to plot our course, continuing slowly and deliberately towards the outline of the Sierras only scant miles away. I knew the entire territory of the region like the back of my hand, and my horse sensed we were one in all that was happening and all that was needed.

We continued on, and on a slightly higher dune I turned on the back of my horse to look back to the village, and noted that several lights had been turned on in the last row of houses in which our home was located. Suddenly I heard a loud call raised by someone in the glimmer of the lights, but too distant to understand. My horse and I continued our wandering from dune to dune, in a silent inner communion as real and understandable as if a lively conversation were going on between us.

Eventually we arrived at another sand dune that afforded a complete view of our village, and now the whole town was lit up, and I could hear the sound of excited voices. In a piercing insight I knew exactly what was going on, but I forced myself to close a wall around what I knew. We continued, and continued, and our communion of souls grew deeper and deeper and ever more satisfying. Eventually I nudged my horse to the side and then into a complete turn, and he knew as I did that it was time to go back home. Then I saw a knot of forms detach itself from the village and begin to move roughly in our direction. I nudged the horse to the left so we would avoid them as they climbed the dunes and we turned towards our home.

Finally we were there, and without any contact with the search party which was already lost in the dunes behind us. We made for the chicken pen become horse pen, and there we said our quiet good night. I slipped quietly into our house and into the room my brothers and I used for our bedroom. It was empty as I knew it would be, and the whole house was dark. I slid under the covers, and shortly I could hear approaching voices headed for our home.

Eventually the principal part of the group left and I heard my parents and brothers coming in the kitchen door. The silhouette of my father passed the bedroom door opening and I heard his intake of breath.

"My God, Peggy, he's here!"

"Yes, I can just see him, and he's sleeping. He needs his sleep. Don't wake him up."

I knew my mother's care had saved me. The next morning all happened as habit always dictated. Not a word was said about the previous night. Not a word was ever said. But I knew what a treasure of companionship the night had brought me.

そ

One of the most important aspects of Don's childhood was his relationship with his dog. In preparation for writing his biography (*An Almost Perfect Balance*), Don wrote to me:

"Denny Brooks Stevens. It is strange how much importance an animal can have on one's development during one's youth. This has always stood out in my mind when, on many occasions, I had reason to remember my first dog, Denny. He was a thoroughbred Scotch collie...

"Denny came into my life on my first birthday, on January 14, 1920. I knew instantly that something unusual and certainly important was happening when I saw my father open the door from the kitchen into the living room where I was sitting propped up on the couch. Dad had a strange grin on his face I had never seen before, and the way he stood was very odd also. His arms were behind his back and he seemed to be holding something there; even as I was trying to relate all this to what little I had at that stage of my life in my memory of my dad's actions, he brought his arms around and I saw he was holding something that looked like a small pillow, but with fur on it, which made no sense. Then he stooped towards the floor and the bundle of fur developed legs and in an instant raced directly towards me.

"I hardly had time to take in all this before the bundle of fur rocketed up onto the couch beside me and knocked me flat onto my back and something wet plastered all over my face. ... Anyway, there it was, my first birthday, and my first dog. I think my father had divine premonition to have captured two such important things together. Denny was unique, but even that I did not know at that time, nor what something unique was, but the word gathered deep meaning as the years rolled along and my first dog taught me so many human things for the first time." One of the only times I saw Don cry was while remembering Denny, and his eventual passing.

During 1923 (as Don said, when he was about five) his family moved to Galt, California (about twenty miles south of Sacramento). A few years later Don's father died of illness. His dear mother subsequently remarried, and Don was fond of his stepfather. Again, for my work on his biography, Don allowed me to ask personal questions, and we are fortunate to have his answers[1]:

Laurent (LW): What did you do in California as a child? Was that move hard on you? Did you spend a lot of time with your brothers? Did you rapidly make new friends?

Don (DES): Remember that when I was seven years old my father died, and the whole family went to work. There was no time for anything other than helping mother in the house and starting raking leaves for neighbors and later studying music. I almost never saw my brothers from this time on as they had their jobs to make money, and we only saw each other at dinnertime. As both went away to university at the age of sixteen, I then saw them only for short times in summer vacations.

I made a lot of friends quite fast as I was smart, and my first idea of finding oneness was to control the other fellow so he was dependent on me. I saw rather soon that this was a totally erroneous idea of satisfying oneness, and 'Mac' in [my] first year of college taught me how erroneous that had been. It was the man in the blue shawl[2] who explained all that to me so I felt it in my bones and felt into a totally new type of oneness with others. This was not easy, as this necessitates the lowering of barriers on both sides, and very few people feel able to do this.

LW: You said that you wrote as a child and got published in one of the small local California town papers. At what age did you start writing work that got published? What was your favorite subject to contemplate and write about when you were younger? What is your favorite subject now

DES: About age ten. Animals. Creation.

ℰↃ

During the 1930s, Don attended Montezuma School for Boys (MSB) in Los Gatos, California (near Santa Cruz). While at MSB, Don met Professor Ernest Andrew Rogers (whom he later referred to as simply "Prof"). Don said Prof was a mystic at heart, but that he never introduced the boys to any particular spiritual path. Prof simply used the phrase "Cosmic Consciousness." Prof singled out Don and shared more personally with him, and gave Don the notion of "True idealism." At that time, Don was involved with church, Sunday School, and sang in the church choir. Don explained directly about that time in his life:

"I would say that by the late teens, I realized that not just physical longing, but an inner need for wholeness, was fundamental and could only be met finally by a long process of understanding why oneness was blocked within us. This is why I became a Sufi and why I understood at once when I first stood before Baba[3] that he had completely answered this need for wholeness, but not to be yet in a permanent and total manner. I was quite content to go through the process of removing the huge internal block that was necessary. I did not resent this nor wish to hurry it in any manner. Just to know that there was a solution and that I had already had a taste of it was enough to be happy and willing to go the course."

After high school, Don attended freshman year at Black

Mountain College in North Carolina. It was an experimental college, and he didn't like their "liberal idealism," leaving after one year to attend Johns Hopkins University (JHU). Don was a member of the Phi Beta Kapa Fraternity, whose principles were: "personal freedom, scientific inquiry, liberty of conscience and creative endeavor."

While Don was a sophomore at JHU, he was a witness to one of Prof's premonitory dreams: In it there was a heavy rainstorm, with mudslides, and the students at Montezuma School would be unable to get food, etc. As a result of the dream, Prof sent a telegram to the school warning of the/a coming storm, and to help the kids, he told the staff to buy extra food and other provisions. As fate would have it, this dream came true, and Prof's intervention made a real difference. This experience made a deep impression on Don, still many years before his initial contact with Meher Baba.

Don spent summers working on his friends the Coles' family farm in New Hampshire. The Coles had also known Ralph Waldo Emerson personally. In 1940, Don graduated from Johns Hopkins University with a degree in Organic Chemistry.

Shortly after graduation, Don's natural curiosity had him commence with "thought-force experiments." This was a type of experiment using mental forces to affect the external world. The results of this proved to Don that it works. During this time he was involved in personal psychological work with Dr. Kathryn Ahlstrand related to his spiritual experimentation. It was Dr. Ahlstrand who introduced him to Murshida Rabia Martin.

Shortly after 1940, Don was initiated by Murshida Martin as a mureed of Hazrat Inayat Khan's Sufi Order in America. Don said he was individually initiated, not in a group setting. The now famous Sufi, Samuel Lewis, was already a member of this order at that time, having met Murshida Martin in 1919. The actual base of her Sufi group at that time was in Fairfax, California. That original center was subsequently sold by Sufism Reoriented, per Meher Baba's direct order, to help fund the publication of *God Speaks*, a decision that upset Sam Lewis deeply.

Don returned to Montezuma School for Boys (MSB) as a teacher of Physics, Chemistry and Mathematics. He then became an official adviser to junior and senior classes at MSB to help them go to University. Of this time, Don said he was interested in a "marriage of science and mysticism."

Soon after, Don became interested in "channeling," and had conversations with the author Stuart Edward White and his deceased wife Betty. Through his advising the students at MSB, Don became friends with oil executives such as Mr. Clarke Gester, Chief Geologist of Standard Oil of California (later Chevron), as well as Mr. Terry Duce, Texaco Representative for Aramco, and also their wives, (who Don said were spiritual), namely Bili Gester, and Ivy Duce.

After two years of teaching and trying to be a surrogate father to the students, Don left Montezuma school. Shortly after, he had an experience one night at the Olympian Hotel (in California) in which he literally was visited by a man with a blue shawl, who guided him spiritually. While Don explained to me that the conversation in the middle of the night was long and thorough, regarding love and companionship (and other topics), it was clear that the man was a disembodied soul. Don wrote a small book about this figure, and there are a few copies of it in private collections.

During 1945, Murshida Martin put her Sufi order directly under Avatar Meher Baba's supervision (a full seven years before Don met Baba in New York in 1952). Francis Brabazon arrived in Fairfax from Australia to prepare for Baba's visit there. Soon after, Murshida Rabia Martin became ill and shared profoundly with Don on her deathbed just before passing. The period from 1945 until 1952 is a transition period during which Ivy Duce became the new Murshida of the order, and Don helped her in the creation and running of the innovative order under Meher Baba's direct guidance.

During 1952, shortly before Don met Baba, a letter came from Baba addressed to him, in which Baba referred to Don as "my son." Unfortunately, Meher Baba was involved in an automobile accident while traveling from Myrtle Beach, South Carolina to Ojai, California, and never got past Oklahoma. Instead, Don traveled to meet Baba in New York at Ivy Duce's Manhattan apartment.

After this initial meeting, another letter came from Baba to Don, this one referring to Don as, "my spiritual son." Meher Baba explained about the "spiritual son" of the Master in *Discourses*[4] in relation to obedience (bold is mine):

For the complete story of Don's first meeting with Baba see: Meher *Baba's Word and His Three Bridges* (London: Companion Books, 2003).

"Such literal obedience is not even bound by the requirement that the real significance of the orders should be within the intellectual comprehension of the pupil, and it is the best type of obedience for which you can aspire. Through such implicit and unquestioning obedience, all the crooked knots of your desires and sanskaras are set straight. It is also through such obedience that a deep link is created between the Master and the pupil, with the result that there is an unhindered and perennial flow of spiritual wisdom and power into the pupil. **At this stage the pupil becomes the spiritual son of the Master, and in due time he is freed from all individualistic and sanskaric ties. Then he himself becomes a Master.**"

Another statement from Baba was that Don had, "An almost perfect balance of head and heart."

At another time, Don wrote to me, "I was reminded by Bal Natu of two brief but very important actions by Baba as he returned from the 1952 visit to the USA and Europe. On his arrival in Zurich after the accident and the final visit to New York, he was sitting in Hedi Mertens' garden with several of the women who accompanied him, including several from the USA to that point. One of them wrote me from Zurich that on this occasion Baba mentioned out of the blue that it had been worth spilling his blood on American soil for the opportunity to meet someone of the caliber of Don Stevens."

Shortly after this, Meher Baba commenced the personal training of Don and the Sufi charges now under the guidance of Ivy Duce. Baba explained what he meant by honesty to the Sufis, a long explanation which made a giant impact on Don's understanding of spirituality. This was to turn into not one but two "vows" of honesty Baba asked of Don, both spiritually and in his work at Chevron.

Next, Baba asked Don and Ivy to edit *God Speaks* for publication. During this period, Baba, Ivy, and Don created Sufism Reoriented, and the correspondence shows that Don stressed the need for "democratic principles." This was considered rather revolutionary by Baba, as he said it had never been done before in a Sufi order.

Don told us directly a great story about what happened next.

Once upon a time, Meher Baba invited the Western male disciples to India for three weeks of special sahavas (which became the *Three Incredible Weeks* visit). Don Stevens was invited but was unable to attend due to illness. He wrote to Baba about this, who responded, "I will make it up to you, Don."

So the next year Baba held the "Four Language Groups Sahavas" for the four main language groups of India. Each language group had one week of sahavas with Beloved Baba. Don was invited to attend that. He was one of only two from the West. Francis Brabazon was the other. Don told me that after the Sahavas, as he was packing to leave, one of the disciples came to his room saying, "Baba is calling you." Don immediately stopped what he was doing, as he had been trained by Baba to do, and followed the Indian disciple out of the building.

Don's version of this story can be found in *Meher Baba's Word and His Three Bridges.*

Don said that right outside the door of his lodging, under the nearest tree, sat Baba in a chair, with a small table next to him. On the table was a stack of papers, and on top of the papers was a rock. Don was surprised by all this, and Baba spoke to him through a disciple, saying something like – Don, I hope you have enjoyed your time here with me, during this sahavas.

Of course Don replied that it was thrilling and lovely, and how happy he was to have been there. Baba continued, gesturing to the papers on the table – I have brought here some of my messages and words given out over the years, which as I have told you in the past, are of the type that I have personally gone over with the Mandali (i.e. Baba's favorite special words of his own). Would you be willing to take these back with you and make something like a little book out of them, similar to *Discourses*?

And with that Baba picked the papers up off the table and held them out to Don.

But Don said – Baba, I don't know how I could do that, those are your words (meaning it was such a grand task to perform).

To which Baba responded, "I will help you."

Don agreed, saying — I will do my best Baba.

And Baba was very happy, and continued, saying something like – And now that you have been here at this sahavas, you could write another part that describes your experiences here. In fact, I have had my secretary keeping careful notes of what I have shared here, and I could make those notes available to you as well. That could be a part of such a book, don't you think?

Don again agreed. Baba continued, and Don, Baba values your own insights and observations, and understanding. You could also be free, and write another section just based on your own feelings about Baba, and spirituality. That would be a good section too, yes? Don agreed, and Baba handed him the papers.

When Don got back to the West, he said he took the papers out of the envelope he had them in, and laid them out around him in subject/topic piles. Then he picked up each pile and read it. He said, amazingly, each pile needed almost no writing from him to glue the passages together into a coherent chapter! He felt this is what Baba meant by, "I will help you." That is Part II of *Listen, Humanity*. Part I is Don's experience of the sahavas. Part III is Don's own feelings about Meher Baba.

As Don was leaving, Baba gave Don a bill for the special room Don used during that Sahavas, which Baba explained was constructed at Meherabad for Don to use. Don paid the bill for the labor and materials. Don made it a point to explain that was how Baba operated, clearly and honestly.

᷍

Another time, on Don's birthday, Baba took off the sadra he was wearing and gave it to his Beloved Mehera, with instructions to keep it for Don, as a birthday gift. The next time Don was at Meherazad to visit Baba, he asked Mehera to bring this gift for Don. Don would travel with this sadra in his suitcase, in a terrycloth bag, and take it out to share with people who came to his Baba talks or seminars. He wanted these items from Baba to be experienced, and as he said, "not kept under glass."

Don said the two things that he tried to work out without Baba's help were "money," and his intimate relationships, until he decided that he couldn't make a worse mess of both, and brought them to Baba, for His guidance. Don said Baba gave him "direct instructions in relation to my deepest and closest relationships at that time."

Around this time, Meher Baba made two references that Don was one of his "close Mandali." One was during 1956 at Meher Mount in California to Bili Eaton,[5] and the other at was at Meherazad, to Eruch.[6] Around this time, Don was asked by Baba to edit Dr.

For more about his relationships see the books *Some Results* (London: Companion Books, 1995) and *Sexuality on the Spiritual Path* (London: Companion Books, 2007) both by Don E. Stevens (and companions).

Deshmukh's five volume version of *Discourses* by Meher Babafor a modern Western audience (such as the new "hippies" in America and Europe). This led to the conversation between Baba and Don about the "atom bombs" of spiritual energy attached by Baba to his own special words.[7] Baba then pointed his finger at Don and told him, "And it is your responsibility to explain to Baba's lovers what I have explained to you today."

Another smaller project that Don undertook for Baba was the editing and publication of his various messages on drugs into a single pamphlet entitled *God in A Pill?*

God in a Pill? was later rewritten and published as *A Mirage Will Never Quench Your Thirst* (Myrtle Beach: Sheriar Foundation, 2003).

It is also important to mention here that before Meher Baba passed away, he gave Don sole responsibility for the translation of his major works into three European languages: Spanish, French and German. These languages were selected by Meher Baba himself in conversation with Don, and by the time I met him for the first time in 2002, these translations were just coming to a place of total completion. For example *God Speaks* is now available in French as *Dieu Parle* (Tredaniel, 1998), in Spanish as *Dios Habla* (Kairos, 2001), and lastly in German as *Der göttliche Plan der Schöpfung* (Ludwig Verlag, 2004). For subsequent translations, such as the Hebrew *God Speaks* by Michal Sivan, Don continued acting as a consultant. In addition to *God Speaks*, translations of Meher Baba's classic *Discourses* were created in French, Spanish, German, and other languages as well. Don took this responsibility very seriously, and I personally worked with him to write up a "Guidelines for Translations" document, which he signed, based on his long conversations with Meher Baba on this subject, and his deep experience in this work.

In the late 1960s, Don eventually came to an impasse with Sufism Reoriented, and wrote a lengthy letter to Meher Baba pouring out his heart about his struggles. In response, not a word came from Meher Baba, but his boss at Chevron suddenly reassigned Don to live and work in Europe!

When I moved to England to work with Don on his biography, and ultimately other projects as well, I asked him: What is it that Don Stevens most deeply wants?[8] He responded:

Oddly enough, neither God-realization nor to be rejoined with Baba. …Baba gave me a glimpse of complete Oneness, and I understand fully that for that to be permanent, I must go through the discipline of wiping out sanskaras, and I have no wish to slight or avoid that in any manner. And to be rejoined with Baba, that is a bit ridiculous, as again he showed me that first day after dropping the body that he was more constantly and closely at my side than he was when his body was sitting over in Meherazad. So, what I find regularly to be the most important thing to me is to live completely honestly and openly with those I love, which is quite a few people, and that I find to be a not-easy-bill to fill. In fact, it is a constant challenge, but I also admit, a delightful challenge.

This period of time in Don's life, from 1969 through the end of his life, started with a project for Chevron with the Spanish government. To quote Don, "I was living in London in early 1969 on indefinite assignment there" by Chevron.[9] And we can see from his writing (in *Tales from the New Life)* that during 1974-75 he was living, at least part-time, in Madrid, Spain.

From this point onwards, Don would move around frequently in Europe to such countries as France, Malta, England, Switzerland, and Monaco, with particular emphasis on England and France, and regular trips to India. Part of his personal financial strategy at this time was to invest the money he was earning from Chevron to assure his comfortable retirement. He decided to take the advice of his partner Claude Longuet, and invest primarily in French real estate. He purchased apartments in Paris and Cagnes sur Mer, and this proved to be quite successful. Not only did he provide a comfortable retirement for himself, but there was enough surplus from the sale of real estate that he could endow Majestic Foundation, an organization he created for Meher Baba work, with ongoing capital.

The legendary rocker Pete Townshend recalls this time in Don's life:

From an article "In Love with Meher Baba," by Townshend which appeared in *Rolling Stone* magazine No. 71 (November 1970).

"Baba Meetings In My Old Flat: In Britain there are fewer Baba lovers. There have been a number of centers in London over the years, but it is only recently that the number of young people becoming interested in Baba indicated a need for a permanent center. The first one that I was involved in was actually one of my old pads. Right in the heart of Soho, it was on the top floor of an office block. It was an incredible experience to walk into the sun streaming up there through big half circle windows, and hear Don Stevens, our London father figure (he's actually from S.F.), give a talk on one of Baba's discourses."[10]

So by November 1970, Don was already looked upon as a London "father figure" in the Meher Baba community. It was during this period that Don began a series of writing projects that would show him as a thought leader in the Baba community, and mystic in his own right. Through deep contemplation, profound intuition, and sharing deeply his spiritual understanding (most of which was an extrapolation of Meher Baba's core concepts), many groups he was involved with in Europe and America flourished.

All books are published by Companion Books unless noted otherwise, and include but are not limited to:

1. *Tales from the New Life with Meher Baba*: Narrated by Eruch, Mehera, Mani and Meheru. Edited by Don E. Stevens (Berkeley: Beguine Library, 1976)

2. *Man's Search for Certainty* (New York: Dodd Mead, 1980)

3. *Listen! The New Humanity* (1985)

4. *The Inner Path in the New Life* (1989)

5. *Some Results* (1995)

6. *Meher Baba, The Awakener of the Age* (1999)

7. *Meher Baba's Word and His Three Bridges* (2003)

8. *Mandali Email*, by Don E. Stevens and Bhau Kalchuri (2005)

9. *Meher Baba's Gift of Intuition,* by Don E. Stevens and Companions (2006)

10. *Sexuality on the Spiritual Path,* by Don E. Stevens with Charles Haynes, et al (2007)

11. *The Doorbell of Forgiveness,* by Don E. Stevens with his Young People's Group (2011)

This period also indicates a shift in Don's work for Meher Baba from a public and international role to one absorbed more in small group work, and focused primarily in Europe and India. To be sure, Don still traveled the world between the 1970s and 2010, but more and more he seemed to be convinced that the spiritual patterns he discerned in Meher Baba's period of activity known as the New Life were to be lived by modern devotees. These patterns included doing spiritual work with a close group of dedicated companions on the Path, and focusing on intuition as a source of Truth, rather than any external (or past) master. Make no mistake, Don loved Meher Baba totally and completely. However, he made it clear to us that Baba was actually more present now, after his physical passing, than he was while he was "in the body."

While some of what Don intuited and shared was highly controversial, there can be no doubt that it was all firmly rooted in his decades-long relationship with and extensive service to Avatar Meher Baba. In fact, he saw the intuitive mechanism as finally giving the seeker direct access to communication with God (or Meher Baba within, after his passing). This is based on what Meher Baba told Don in Mandali Hall at Meherazad in the 1960s, which is that in this Avataric manifestation period, as in all Avataric periods, the Avatar gives a "gift" to humanity.

Apparently Baba explained all the previous Avataric gifts, and said that as Meher Baba his gift to humanity is that of intuition. This is documented, and we explored this thoroughly, in the book *Meher Baba's Gift of Intuition.* Don was extremely reluctant to attribute any of his own intuitive sessions to Meher Baba, except on rare occasions when he said it was the same manner of communication that he was so used to experiencing with Baba, when he was alive in the body. Don was hyper-sensitive to the potential dangers of attributing intuitions directly to Meher Baba. He had seen this done throughout his life, by many Baba lovers, even including Mandali, and he felt it was important to "true" intuitions with a circle of close spiritual companions, a major topic of the intuition book.

This period after Don's life in America, and starting with the small groups in Europe, can also be seen as a major shift away from his work to found and co-create with Meher Baba and Ivy Duce the exoteric organization known as Sufism Reoriented, to the more intimate and esoteric (even mystical) work which had – no organization – and which was focused on inner spiritual experience. Much can be said about this; however this introduction could never contain a full treatment of these topics. Suffice it to say that a sentence or two about each of Don's books which appear in this period could shed sufficient light in the long hallway he was so sure lead to God's Door:

Tales from the New Life.

Because of a somewhat heroic act which Don had performed, Eruch said, "Don, for that, I will finally tell you what you have been asking me for so long to tell, the story of our New Life with Meher Baba." It was in the hearing of these tales that Don first glimpsed the real work he felt Baba had done for the New Humanity. That was, to lay down new patterns and archetypes for spiritual seekers, away from the guru-disciple relationship, and towards a model of spiritual companionship. Intuition will be the primary guide, in relationship with the Avatar, and with the presence of a living Elder Brother (or Sister) to help "true" the intuitions.

Man's Search for Certainty, and *Listen! The New Humanity.*

Here Don first lays out his observations regarding what humanity needs, especially in this Avataric age, in order to find real fulfillment. This is based on his direct experience under Baba's spiritual guidance, and marks Don's first real foray into the subjects with Baba as the internal guide. We can see Don experimenting with all that he has experienced in over sixty years of his earthly career, both humanly and spiritually, and trying to find the best way forward, not just for himself, but for the New Humanity, which he felt was here on earth now. These books are about Don's feelings of what we should be, and will be doing, spiritually.

The Inner Path in the New Life.

This book marks Don's sense of certainty that Meher Baba's "Last Message on the Alphabet Board" was not just a message, but a giant clue in the mystery of how humanity is supposed to behave now that the Avatar has moved off the earthly stage. To quote from that message, as Don frequently did, "…This will enable all persons to realize Truth by being bound to each other with internal links." This statement about the inner links between spiritual companions, and their importance, was returned to throughout the years by Don. How exactly these internal links are forged by the Avatar, and each one of us, and then maintained (or broken), and their relationship to the realization of Truth, was a subject that became somewhat of an obsession for Don.

Some Results.

This book shows a deepening conviction that the Manifestation that Baba promised had indeed taken place – as Don felt that Baba had actually manifested in the 1960s. The "results" Don shared in this book are similar to what he had been sharing in previous publications, but with a greater clarity and intention towards self-revelation. Where in the past he had been more guarded about his personal life, he now becomes almost entirely transparent, towards a sense of Oneness with the reader.

Meher Baba, The Awakener of the Age.

Don explained this book was not his idea, but a request of the Spanish publisher of *God Speaks.* They felt it would be better to sell *Dios Habla* to a Spanish public that knew something of Meher Baba, but there was nothing yet available in Spanish. Don wrote this biography of Meher Baba based on his enormous personal experience with Baba. Don told me he relived many of the experiences with Baba while writing this, and realized how much physical intimacy he received from Baba in the way of hugs, kisses on the cheek and neck, and handholding over the years. He attributed this Avataric affection with the wiping out of his sanskaras of lust.

From 2003 until Don's passing in 2011, Don and I worked on five more books together. Don used to tell us that there were three bridges back to God. One, and the most important, is the Avatar himself—known this time as Meher Baba. The second bridge is "The Mandali," those men and women who had totally and completely surrendered their lives to Meher Baba, obeying him implicitly, and whom he invited to live and work with him. Baba took total responsibility for their lives. While there were a few "Western Mandali," Baba almost never indicated who they were. The third bridge, he said, was "Baba's Word."

Don decided in late 2003 that he would rededicate himself to working with the younger generation, which he said he had not done since the 1960s. Together we created a list of Baba young adults around the world and invited them to what he at first called a "Carry the Torch" seminar. He said he wanted to pass the torch of wisdom and understanding he had received from Avatar Meher Baba to these people. After much consideration, we agreed that he would also pick four couples, which he called Godparents, and visit their homes in America, so that the young adults could come and hear what he wanted to share. This became Don's Young People's Group (YPG). He did this ten times. The first was in February, 2004, near Los Angeles, and then continued over the next six years in Oregon, Massachusetts, the Meher Baba Center in South Carolina,

Georgia, and lastly in New Hampshire. Each time it was an opportunity for Don to pass on what he felt Baba had given to him. The seventh such YPG gathering is captured in the book *The Doorbell of Forgiveness*.

Bruce Milburn explained to me many times that Don's work with small groups in London and France started in the 1970s, and for decades were faithfully tended to by Don on a monthly basis. Bruce experienced this careful attention from Don first hand. By 2003, Don was publishing a schedule of his travels and providing it to the group members so that they would know exactly when he planned to be where. Based on this pattern, he would visit London, Paris, the south of France, India, America, and other places, until he simply could no longer travel due to old age.

Another example of Don's Baba work was in the summer of 1988, a three-day seminar conducted by him on the subject of "sanskaras."[11] It was attended by more than thirty people in the south of France. Such a gathering, for people of different nationalities, epitomized the tone and intention of Don: to bring lovers of Meher Baba (and God) together to contemplate deeply the most important spiritual subjects of the time. According to Baba, never before had the Avatar given so much detail about spiritual subjects, such as sanskaras, as found in *God Speaks* and *Discourses*. Here was Don taking it all terribly seriously, and prodding humanity to action. One South African Baba lover, now living in California, who knew and loved Don, told me that Baba had said, "Don will give love like a philanthropist gives money." From the accounts I have heard first hand, as well as those published, and my own personal experience and observations, this was absolutely true.

Once in London when Don and I were comparing notes about how we related to Meher Baba in our spiritual lives, Don explained, "I just try to bring as much love as I can into every interaction that I have." Don was extremely strong in mind as well as heart, and he would frequently remind those who attended any Baba group meeting of the importance of the balance of mind and heart. To this end, I started collecting quotes from Meher Baba about this subject:

> "I repeat, materialism and spirituality must go hand in hand. The balance of head and heart must be maintained; the head for discrimination, and the heart for feeling, whereby it is possible to realize infinite consciousness in art, science, nature and in every phase of life." ~ Meher Baba[12]

In 2004, during a period of international travel, or "going about my father's business" as Don called it, he confided in me about what his cardiologist had said to him. Don needed a heart-valve replacement surgery. Don asked me what I felt should be done, given his age (at the time he was in his mid-80s). After researching heart-valve replacement surgery (which is obviously highly invasive), I said that I didn't feel it was wise, given the risks, and the long convalescence process. He agreed. It was only two years after that conversation, while in Salem, Massachusetts indeed Don's heart couldn't keep up, and he was rushed to the hospital with congestive heart failure. In fact, he died in the ambulance, and they instantly revived him just in time for emergency care. He subsequently received the heart surgery in Salem, and lived five more years.

Don told me it was Sevn McAuley who saved his life. Dan Sanders, who was also present, recalls: "Don knocked on Sevn's door to tell him he couldn't breathe, at 3am. This woke me up. I woke the Griffins who called 911, as Sevn helped Don sit down. Don credited Sevn with saving his life by giving the paramedics key information about Don's heart condition in the ambulance. Sevn was the only one of us in the ambulance with Don."

Two final topics must be covered here in relation to Don's life. The first is what came to be known as Beads on One String, and the other is the importance of forgiveness, after which I will simply refer you to Don's upcoming biography, *An Almost Perfect Balance*.

Two things happened around 2003 that convinced Don of the importance of interfaith work: First Carl Ernst, came from America and gave a talk at the London Meher Baba Centre, and we spoke to him at length after this at Don's flat, about Islam and Sufism.

Then in 2004, we did the first Beads on One String pilgrimage tour of the places that Baba had indicated to Don were special "focal points" of spiritual energy in India. Some of these points were related to past Avataric Advents, or Perfect Masters,

Carl W. Ernst is the Kenan Distinguished Professor of Islamic studies at the Department of Religious Studies at the University of North Carolina at Chapel Hill.

and some were related to Meher Baba's own work. Upon return to London from India, Don had to recuperate in the hospital due to severe dehydration. While in the hospital he had an intuition clearly showing him that the reason Baba himself visited these spiritual places was because of the need to tear down the walls of separateness and hatred between faiths. The New Humanity would live in harmony with all faiths together, as Baba had said, "like beads on one string."

What had been to Don in the past merely a nice poetic phrase suddenly came to life as one of Baba's greatest works in his lifetime, bringing these faiths together in Oneness and love. It became a sudden and deep motivation which would last many years, and he continued to personally take Baba lovers on Beads on One String pilgrimage tours in India and Europe until he was too old to travel.

Lastly, for about ten years (between 2001 and the end of his life), Don received intuitions about the importance of forgiveness. During our October 2007 Young People's Group weekend gathering, Don had the whole weekend focused on this topic, and we explored it thoroughly. This was a period when Baba groups were fighting amongst themselves, and this pained Don greatly.

I was with Don in California again as a Baba group was going through their process to sort out internal problems. Don had come all the way from London to be present and provide his support to all sides of the altercation, but specifically to sit next to one member of the group. At that time Don asked me to continue the forgiveness work, especially with this specific Baba group, and said, "Forgiveness is the most important spiritual work in the world today." That was the last time I saw my Big Bear, Don.

Beloved Baba, thank you for allowing me to know, work, and play with this spiritual son of yours. May he indeed be with you again, behind the door that leads to God, at the end of that hallway you walked along with him.

End Notes:

1. From my unpublished research, *"DonAnswersMoreQuestions.doc."*

2. The "Man in the blue shawl" is a reference to a spiritual experience Don had years before meeting Meher Baba, where he received guidance from a man who appeared to him one night. He wrote a booklet, self-published, with the same title.

3. That first meeting was in New York in 1952.

4. See *Discourses*, by Meher Baba, 6th edition, Volume I, page 90: "The Removal of Sanskaras: III".

5. The incident with Bili Eaton I personally confirmed with Bili, via telephone in New York, and she said, "But Don wouldn't care about that." It is an unpublished account.

6. The incident with Baba and Eruch is published in *Lord Meher*, p. 6289: http://www.lordmeher.org/index.jsp?pageBase=page.jsp&nextPage=6289

7. For this story, see *Meher Baba's Word and His Three Bridges* (London: Companion Books, 2003).

8. Ibid, Don Answers.

9. See *The Inner Path in the New Life*, (Inner Path) p. 31.

10. The *Rolling Stone* article can be found online at http://www.thewho.net/articles/rs_1970.htm (accessed July 2013).

11. Ibid, Inner Path, "Inner Path, Out of Reach" by R. Mehrabanpour, p. 94.

12. May 19, 1932, in New York, from a (two page) printed message given to reporters
    who came on board the ship "Bremen"; See: *Lord Meher*, pp.1616-1618. (www.lordmeher.
    org/index.jsp?pageBase=page.jsp&nextPage=1616); also see *The Perfect Master* by C.
    Purdom, pp.165-168, and *Messages of Meher Baba, East and West,* Adi K. Irani (ed.) pp.
    84-87.

Introduction

By Wayne Smith

Somewhere in the early summer of 2009 I had just completed the recording of an interview with Don Stevens when he mentioned an idea that he was keen to discuss. It concerned the placing in the public domain of a book, one that would present some of those issues that had concerned Don over the years and which he, having just turned ninety, would be able to respond to while he was still with us. At that point I had already been interviewing Don for several years in relation to his biography, a project that was overseen by Laurent Weichberger (a companion of Don's from the USA), and which involved several other people working on different themes and areas of Don's life.

I don't think when any of us started this undertaking that we realised just how vast the project would be and how long it would take, for Don's life had been so long and eventful, one in which he had known and made lasting friendships with countless people, both through his life in the oil business and in his spiritual endeavors as a practicing Sufi and follower of Meter Baba. In 2009 the project had already been in process for the better part of a decade, and it seemed likely that the better part of another would still be needed. It was for this reason, and the fact that Don was not becoming any younger, that he decided an initial volume of the biography should be put into the public domain as soon as possible. It was agreed that we would start the process later in the year, after the summer break.

The format and procedure for these interviews followed the same pattern that we had established over the several years I had been interviewing and recording Don for the biography. That is, they would take place at the 228 Hammersmith Grove flat where he stayed while he was in London and where I would meet him after travelling down from my home in the Welsh Marches the previous evening. Usually I would arrive at the flat on the morning of the Saturday, around 9 - 9.30 am, and spend anywhere between an hour and an hour-and-a-half interviewing Don, before other companions started to arrive for the meeting of the "Saturday Group" to which we both belonged.

This always felt like a special, sacred kind of time for me: the two of us together; myself witnessing this ninety-year-old man opening up and moving back into a past and a life lived as richly and as deeply as perhaps any life could be. Don's ability to recount in exact detail moments and experiences was extraordinary, and on more than one occasion, whilst remembering people and places that had been especially dear to him, he would be so moved that the recording had to be halted. You see, Don had such a warm affection for so many people, both living and departed, that he was frequently overwhelmed by his memories and recollections of them.

When it came to the material for this new book (whose initial working title was "Volume 1" ... "Volume 2" being the biography proper), the interviews felt more structured and formal than those I had previously been involved in, as if Don had a strict agenda and was perhaps aware that time was more pressing than it had been before. This surmise was confirmed for me after his death when Sevn McAuley (a close friend and travelling companion of Don's in his later years) passed on to me a handwritten note on which Don had indeed scribbled down a list of the topics that he had wished to broach.

The first of these interviews took place on December 19, 2009, and the last on September 25, 2010, a month before Don suffered the fall in his Paris flat that would subsequently lead to his diminishing health and demise the following April. At the end of this final session, Don hinted that one more might be necessary, but alas it was never to be and its subject matter remains a persistent mystery to this day. For when I tried to arrange another

interview with Don on his return to London in January of 2011,
he firmly but politely declined, his reason being that his limited
energies could stretch only as far as being able to present and
discuss some "recent intuitions" that he'd had while convalescing in
France. Sadly this meeting would turn out to be the last occasion
on which I would see Don alive.

Back in 2009, arriving on that autumn morn, I already had
preconceptions about some of the "sensitive issues" that Don
mentioned he might want to cover, for it was the case that he had
alluded to several over the years that I had been working on his
biography, and in my role as Chairman of Companion Books (a
publishing company that Don had founded). We also discussed
some within the aforementioned Saturday Group and during
the editorial meetings for the Neti Neti Meher Baba newsletter
in which we were both involved (alongside Renate Moritz, Jane
Hoskin, Carol Pullen, Bruce Milburn and David Lee).

However, I wasn't expecting or had been prepared for what Don
launched into straight away at that first interview: his account of
some "visions" he'd had which he eventually entitled The Three
Snapshots of Reality. I found this to be completely new territory.
I had been used to Don in the past talking about people and
places relating to the biography, but now I had to feel my way
into responding and asking questions in a quite different manner,
as Don painstakingly tried to put on record these very subjective
experiences which quite clearly from the outset were of vital
importance to him.

I must admit that at first I was quite guarded, for Don had
always played down the role and importance of the visionary
experiences that can occur on the spiritual path, especially those
of the occult variety. He had also emphasized to us how important
"truing" intuitions within a trusted companion group should be,
especially if they were to be placed in the public domain. However,
as far as I know, this process doesn't seem to have been the case for
what he labelled his visions. Saying that, there can be no doubt of

both the importance of these experiences for Don and how keen he was to have them expressed and understood as correctly as possible — shown by the fact that he felt it necessary to keep coming back to add to them in the three subsequent interviews that took place. It was as if the process of retelling them was, for Don, a truing process in itself.

The main reason for this, I think, is that it ultimately helped him to understand one of the main conundrums that had perplexed him almost from the very beginning of his spiritual life with Meher Baba: how some of those closest to the Avatar could have acted at times in ways that to Don seemed so un-spiritual. In short, it was the realization that they too not only had sanskaras (impressions) still left to work through, but knots of such perplexity that only the Avatar (the "Master Mechanic" as Don referred to him here) could deal with. However, that's not to say that these close ones were completely mired in a sanskaric mess, for Don considered them only a gossamer veil or two away from Realization itself and often he referred to them in ways that showed how spiritually aware they must have been. Also we shouldn't misunderstand Don's relationship with them: it was only because he loved and felt so close to these people, more than virtually anybody else he had known in his life, that this issue hurt and perplexed him so much, right up till even his experience of the visions themselves.

Furthermore, my understanding from what Don gave, both in this interview and elsewhere, is that he also included himself as a person who had started this lifetime with such deep sanskaric knots that only the personal touch of the Avatar himself could loosen them. He had already mentioned on several public occasions the "worry sanskara" that seems to have afflicted him greatly prior to his coming into Meher Baba's orbit. And midway down, on page four of these transcriptions, he alludes to past "impulsions" and his own experience of the Avatar becoming involved in them.

On another note, I find it interesting that when I questioned

Don about his description of the vision in "Snap One," he referred to the endlessly rolling landscape of the Midwestern prairies as being the "closest thing I ever saw to that." These images from his past may also feature to some degree or another in some of Don's writings, for example in his later intuitions where he refers to, among other things, the "black skillet."

The rest of the interviews are taken up with themes and issues that Don has made many of us familiar with over the years, both in his writings and in the group meetings and seminars he participated in and led. Themes such as those relating to matters of honesty, the karma of finance, how we relate to our own bodies on the spiritual path, the relationship between head and heart, Don's experience of Western Sufism, and his thoughts on Meher Baba's "Manifestation" are covered with Don's careful attention. The final interview concerns Don's relationship with a close Mandali of Baba's, Bhau Kalchuri, and its inclusion here will hopefully lay to rest any abiding questions about what Don referred to as the "so-called differences of opinion between Bhau and Don, which are apparently pretty notorious among Baba lovers."

The presentation of the interviews here in a transcription format is as Don suggested. I had asked him at some stage how he foresaw the book and about the process of writing them up and he said he thought that, with a little "tidying up," they could be presented "... just as they are." Fortunately Don's conversational style lends to this: that is an ability, honed over a lifetime of seminars and meetings, to express himself logically in a prose-like manner; quite often using fully formed sentences that are so well structured and grammatically correct that they require little or no editing to have them make sense on the printed page. It may also be that Don, being aware that this material was ultimately for the public record, answered my questions with this in mind right from the outset. This wouldn't surprise me, and in retrospect now I feel this probably to be the case.

In this process of tidying up, I have tried to remain as faithful as possible to what I feel Don would have wanted, while also appreciating that one of the original intentions of this publication was to create the opportunity for him to respond to any questions that the subject matter might have raised, I have also tried to retain and, hopefully, give a flavor of the actual interviews themselves. Where Don has paraphrased himself or others, I have used inverted commas for clarity of presentation. However, the reader needs to be reminded, particularly in respect to Meher Baba's words, that these are paraphrases and are not meant to represent the exact words of the persons themselves. Where edits occur I have shown this by a series of three dots (...). Furthermore, I have left in many of the breaks and interruptions which were an unavoidable aspect of interviewing Don at this time of day. For with the arrival of others, one by one, for the aforementioned group meeting, Don would politely ask them to wait in the adjoining bedroom if he had something important that he needed to finish. Or, if we had arrived at a natural conclusion and it was approaching the meeting time anyway, he would decide to break off for that session and expect things to be resumed on the next occasion, even if it was some months away. And on the occasions when Claude Longuet (a close friend of Don's) was also present in the flat, it wasn't uncommon for there to be a halt in proceedings whilst Claude raised some important question — usually of a culinary nature in relation to lunch — and typically with a distinct volume from one of the adjacent rooms.

And finally, although a lot of the material covered important and quite serious matters, there was always the opportunity for the lighter side to emerge when conversing with or interviewing Don. This sometimes arose from the least likely of topics, and those who knew him well will have witnessed how his particular sense of humor could express itself at any time and from anywhere, within a range that extended from a wry smile and a witty aside, to a long drawn-out anecdote resulting in the slap of a knee and copious tears of laughter.

THREE SNAPSHOTS OF REALITY
December 19, 2009

Snapshot One

*D*on E. Stevens (DES): All right, I think that how we go about the first part is extremely important for this little first volume, and with its subject matter to be properly presented and appealingly presented. The one thing that has run through my mind is that I simply start with this daytime 'vision' … I don't know what else to call it. I'm not a person who has visions. In fact, I've never had anything in my life by any stretch of the imagination I could call a vision, and yet I was walking up the street … God knows where, somewhere … I don't even remember where I was now …

Wayne Smith (WS): Were you not in Paris, Don?

DES: Okay, all right, so it was still fresh enough that I had a little bit of the surroundings still dangling around. Well, I'm glad to know that. It certainly didn't particularly seem to be Paris.

WS: Unless that was something else you were talking about?

DES: I just don't know; I frankly don't know. But I have never had, let's say, something that was so terribly, terribly visual and just blocked out the whole landscape. And I think I even continued walking and didn't feel at all disoriented or upset by having this — maybe I was subconsciously aware of where I was walking and was doing it sensibly.

WS: It'll be those old physical sanskaras that keep you … make you able to move.

DES: Well, it was certainly automatic and nothing that had volition, because I was so captured by each of these snapshots as they came, that I had absolutely no room even to say, "My God, what's going on here?" It was just so vivid and so important and so riveting.

WS: So this is back in maybe November 2009 this year?

DES: Oh well, it was this year. This was only a few weeks ago. You know, this is still just getting absorbed by Don Stevens.

WS: Did you experience things like lights and those kind of features that people experience ...?

DES: No, I just knew. And how under the sun, for instance, I could know that I was looking at the enormity of God's infinite consciousness I don't know. I don't know what it looked like. I just knew that I was surrounded by, and staring at, a sample of just the vast — extending into God knows where, off, off through the high horizons and all over — just this infinite, infinite unconscious consciousness. I'd say latent consciousness ... I guess that's the way we have to refer to it.

WS: Yes.

D: Yes, I knew. I knew I was right in the centre of it and it was just everywhere, and it went off to the horizons and it was so tremendously complex - there was all of the complexity and all of the simplicity of infinitude.

WS: As part of the created world as well, in the vision?

DES: There was nothing that suggested anything. This was just right buried in infinite latent, plus manifest consciousness ... the state of God ... as it is now. And how much of the infinitude has been converted to manifest, I wouldn't have ... You know, there was nothing that said, "This parcel is manifest; this part over here is still unconscious, latent."

WS: Indivisible to some extent?

DES: Absolutely. I just knew I was right in the middle of the infinitude of God's consciousness, latent and manifest. That was it. And it was just staggering. You know, I've talked an awful lot about just what tremendous newness has to be involved in this business of going from one Cycle of Cycles to a different Cycle of Cycles. And I said the only thing when I get myself down to it and think about it ... it is something like homesteading was in the prairies of the United States for decades, when the government would open up a whole new area of prairie land to homesteading. And when the damn pistol banged, you lit out like hellfire to the place that you thought [you wanted], and put down your stakes, and that's you. It's your claim. And you hope somebody else didn't have his eye on that particular little parcel and get there before you did. There must have been some real fights going on …

WS: Sure, turf wars …

DES: But there are no remaining histories about contention and dissension and injury and shootings or anything of that sort. I was in the middle of this — I mean that's the only thing I can compare it to — just my imagination of what homesteading must have been.

WS: Did it have a feeling aspect to it, the experience?

DES: I didn't feel anything, I just … it was enormity personified. Real, real … a beginning taste of what infinitude means and how enormous infinitude is —it's got everything in it. Chock-a-block!

WS: One would hope so!

DES: Well, one would certainly hope so! If it's gotta be everything, well … {Laughter}. You see these three snapshots are in very recent weeks.

WS: So I think I was confused when I mentioned "on the streets of Paris" in relation to that original intuition you had, about how you're going to go about these things. Then this vision you've had must have been something more recent than that?

DES: Oh, it's terribly recent, it's been in the last two, three weeks.

WS: So that could be in London, it could be anywhere …?

DES: Anywhere, I just don't know. It was so, so real and important that it wiped out everything associated with it.

WS: Gave you a bigger perspective on things …?

DES: Oh, it was, it was … I just knew it was Truth.

WS: Yes.

DES: After all, God's infinite consciousness is a pretty big package. It was just boggling. I didn't know how I even got the right even to see a peek at it.

WS: So how will that relate to what we're doing with this project, do you think?

DES: Well, [snapshot] number two was the drop-soul coming through the Om Point. [Snapshot] number three was the tremendous complexity, particularly because each drop-soul has its own personal Whim, and you never know what a whim is doing. Baba defines it clearly: there's no logic at all. And so if it's the Whim that gets entangled in your personal supply of God's latent infinite consciousness (which is your responsibility to shepherd through the awakening and manifesting stage), boy you've got a pretty big problem on your hands ... what's that damn Whim gonna dream up next!

WS: Yes, which direction is it gonna go ... ?

DES: And so, things can — because it really is true creativeness, unfettered creativeness — and that can get into, let us say, inevitably your mind just looking at the mathematical probability. I said, my God, every once in a while a personal whim is going to dream up a series of things to wake up this particular spoonful of infinite consciousness — a series of experiences that are going to be so damn complex with sanskaric energy compulsion patterns that are gonna be God-awfully difficult to get rid of one day.

And so then number three was just suddenly realizing that that does happen, and realizing that this is probably the most important, major responsibility of the Avatar: to take on these people. And of course we've always looked at the Mandali as being super special people who are terribly advanced—and, you know, just practically next door to being angels and God himself — and instead what they are is the residues of the problem children.

WS: So they're hard nuts to crack.

DES: Very hard nuts to crack. But the important thing to get over in our discussion together is that they are not nasty. They have already had to go through, let's say, the primitive stages of complexity (in other words, anger, bitterness and things of that sort) and they're just plain stuck and doing their damnedest to try to stay afloat. And then along comes the Avatar [who] gives a helping hand, and gives them some responsibilities every once in a while in relation to his infinite Universal Work. And so "occupational therapy" takes over, and their mind is diverted to that, and is creating and fascinated. And so he creeps in the back door while their centre of attention is occupied with that, and starts doing some unwinding.

That's what he did with me. And I realized this when I went back and took a look at … when I had to write that biography [of Meher Baba, which also focused on my relationship with Baba] for the people in Barcelona … and I realized, "My God, when I check back where certain of these impulsions in me are now compared to where they were twenty years ago, I haven't touched them in between time. I haven't had time! They haven't been interesting. And now I see, my God, the energy content and so on is totally different." So I know from my own experience that when the Avatar gets you involved, for whatever reason, in some of his Universal Work, by God, if there's something to be tinkered with in your mental storehouse, he's got free access to it. And because you've surrendered to him, he's got the moral right to tinker. So it all makes sense.

WS: Do you think maybe that working on that group of people — the Mandali — that Baba's also working out and sort of working on other areas of humanity through them: that working with their types, their problems, it's also helping others?

DES: I think this business of consciousness is so unique that that is a minor, minor factor, I really do. In other words, it is a very specialized handling of an absolutely individual drop-soul's consciousness.

WS: Do you think someday that everybody will eventually have that relationship with the Avatar in time, or that there are just groups of people here and there?

DES: No, absolutely not, it's just the ones who statistically get into such a series of tight sanskaric knots that they've got to have help to get out of it.

WS: Specialist Avataric help ...

DES: It takes the guy with the job description who's the Master Mechanic, and that's what the Avatar is. He's the Master Mechanic of Creation and he's got to do it.

January 23, 2010

WS: So Don, it's 2010, January the twenty third, and we're here at session two of the recordings that we started to make in December last year.

DES: Of the first volume, so-called, of the biography, which I dictate direct to you.

WS: That's right, and I send to Kathy to transcribe.

DES: Great. Well, I've made the decision I would like to put before you and Kathy and Sevn and whoever else ... a title for the first volume. And I would simply like to entitle it by that thing that happened to me which set the stage for all of this and which I've been calling: "Three Snaps of Reality." But I think [making] a slight change and calling them "Three Snapshots of Reality" would make it more lucid and clear, because snaps can be many different things.

WS: It's an intriguing title as well. People would look at that and think, well, what's that all about?

DES: Yes. I have to do a typical Stevens here though, and that is start out with my own personal reaction to what happened to me on that occasion, because I think most people would say that it was a psychic or a mystic or a spiritual experience, and all of those terms happen to be very repugnant to me, always have been. So I just have to admit that when this particular incident happened (I was walking somewhere in a city) ... it had to be either Paris or London, and quite frankly the experience was so total and really so hazy that I've never been able to decide whether it was more likely to have been Paris or London. I could probably triangulate and figure out by expense accounts of where I had to be, (when it occurred), but quite frankly I just have always had a deep scepticism and distrust of so-called mystic experiences. And although I have a number of my closest friends who do have them (and even say regularly to me [that] Meher Baba said so-and-so to me; Meher Baba just told me such-and-such and so on, and I love them dearly), I've told them I think once, maybe even twice, that I am not keen on direct contacts nor, above all, efforts to contact Meher Baba directly after he dropped his body. And though I always remain deeply anti-mystic/psychic/spiritual experiences, this was so key, and I've never had one like this, to be quite honest ...

... I was walking, and suddenly, I was not in the city, but I was on — I can't even describe the landscape — I would say [it was] low, undulating, and there was a sense of complexity about that landscape which was not apparent at all. And what I remember of the landscape ... it just looked like undulating, slow hills. I don't think there was even scrub brush growing on it to complicate it. And yet I knew, inside of myself, that in some manner or another, this was meant for me, to give me an idea of the enormity of God's infinitude. And just looking at that ceaseless, endless, rolling hill landscape ... some of it was up and some of it was down; some of it was valley, and some of it was crested hills and so on ... there was nothing spectacular which set off one part of it from another, but it all had character. It all had form. It was just ... I knew that this was as close to a pictorial representation of God's infinitude as it was possible for me to get, and it was just absolutely, utterly, overwhelming.

WS: So you had a feeling experience, as well as a visual one, of being overwhelmed?

DES: Immediately, immediately, that was the essence: that I had never had this concept of the infinitude of God before. I have been used [to the concept of infinity] for many years, because I was a minor in mathematics in my university career, so infinitude was something that I'd dealt with in various matters (and of course I've been familiar with the fact that Baba said that one of the characteristics of God—the original, original state of God — was His infinitude. So it's not new to me). And also, for several years now, I have been very struck, much more struck, by the concept that what Meher Baba has been doing in the Cycle of Cycles of Avataric incarnations, that this must be then the opening up of a new Cycle of Cycles of Avataric incarnations. That this must be a newness of God's infinitude that is being exposed, to be brought from the latent to a manifest state through being, let's say, attached to various drop-souls — the infinitude of drop-souls coming through the Om Point.

And that has always just seemed indelibly clear to me: that the purpose of all of that, the function of all of that, is to carry the latencies of God to a manifest, living state. And also on even such a popular subject as love, I think, it has become very apparent to many of us, that love certainly was not a living property of God in the Beyond-Beyond state, original state of God … that it had to be part of the latency. (I hope your latest edition of your population chart shows that clearly!) {Don is referring here to a chart that Wayne had been working on for years about the qualities latent in God} … But even such an important thing as love (which we all seem to be in total agreement is one of the most incredibly important parts of God' nature, of Creation and of human functioning), that even that was a latency in the original, original state of God.

WS: At this point, Don, you must have maybe just stopped still and had this experience?

DES: I don't know what happened to my walking … I might have gone on walking. I was absolutely, totally unconscious of where I was and what I had been doing. I was totally absorbed in this nondescript, incredibly expansive landscape. I couldn't even see a horizon to it. It was just obvious that it rolled on and it rolled on and it rolled on.

WS: And you were saying that you think this relates to infinite consciousness?

DES: It's related to the infinitude of God; consciousness is only one of its aspects. So it just struck me … I had never got even close, I realized … I just stared, overwhelmed by the immensity. I knew there was no end to it. It just rolled on like that, ad infinitum.

WS: And your feelings of being overwhelmed, what words would you relate to those?

DES: That I was just enormously happy that it was like that. And that I could grasp the enormity of [it]. It was a whole new experience of the sub, sub, sub … the basic substrata of God — the enormity of the infinitude of God. Nothing I've ever thought or imagined even approached it. There it was … wham! It hit me.

WS: So you'd been reading and thinking and discussing this concept of infinitude for many, many years, and all of a sudden it's there, in an [experiential]way.

DES: I haven't discussed too much, even in groups, until recently, in trying to get over to [people the idea] in group activity that this change (the ending of a Cycle of Cycles, and the starting of a new Cycle of Cycles) involves a newness of experience in living forms such as nobody has ever had before. And that is the closest thing to a discussion of infinitude … I don't think I tried to equate that with the infinitude of God in any way before, because this is still (as far as I can tell and I think I've tried to make it clear) enormous and it is totally new. And the things that will be characteristic of it have never been experienced before. It's a new … the non-repetitiveness of God's consciousness to me is a terribly important thing … So it has to be a newness that is just absolutely striking. So the newness is infinite in that sense: that there ain't nothing like it before and will never be [again], because when that part of God's latent consciousness becomes manifest and an Avatar finishes off the accounts, then it becomes permanently a part of God's living, manifest, infinite consciousness.

WS: Individualized?

DES: Yes, but [even] so in that sense there is an aspect of infinitude to it. But it certainly is not in relation to … that is not an infinite part of God's latent consciousness. It is a restricted, definitely sign-posted, if you want to put it that way, area for this new Cycle of Avataric Cycles to bring latent consciousness to manifest consciousness.

WS: So a very important aspect to this experience, this vision, Don, is this newness?

DES: The newness, yes. The newness has an aspect almost of infinitude, but this new area of God's latent consciousness is not infinite; it is definitely circumscribed with boundaries to it. And when it has been all brought to a manifest living state, then it is permanently and endlessly, completely fused into God's infinite consciousness.

WS: So this'll be the next Cycle of Cycles?

DES: Yes, the newness is associated with the next Cycle of Cycles. So it's a part of this sort of rolling brown hills which is now open to humanity to turn it into forests, and parks and sea and whatever not.

WS: Have you any thoughts on what might be the aspects of that new cycle, that newness, that we're on the threshold of — I suppose, unity of life is something Baba has mentioned?

DES: Well, to me, the thing that strikes me most so far has been the newness of the manner of handling esoteric energy, spiritual energy, that's involved in the manner of Baba setting up what I call the Avataric power points in India — those places that have been incorporated into that itinerary called the Beads itinerary now. The manner of passing on the energy is just totally new. I mean once you see what Baba has done, and how he has combined it with the resident spiritual energy of

devotion of the religious faiths that founded that site, and how
he has amalgamated the two...it's logical. And it is not infinitely
large; it is a helluva great big quantity of spiritual energy that's
available there, but it is still not infinite by any means. And the
manner of passing it on, where apparently devotees of the Avatar
in some fashion consciously regard themselves as being a part of
a mechanism for tapping that energy and getting it available ...
And then presumably the Avatar, or somebody in the spiritual
hierarchy of already perfected souls, directs it where it has got to
go and be used.

So all of this fits into common concepts, but still this is an
absolutely — as far as I've been able to see — a completely new
manner of directing energy. It doesn't mean that it has not always
existed (that when you bow down at a venerated place that you
receive some important reactions from that place), but to use it
as a major tool of spiritual development in order to decrease the
over-identification, apparently, that has gone on for centuries
in relation to personality, place, name, philosophy, specific
philosophy. It certainly looks like if anything is ever going to
make a dent in that over-identification, it should be what Baba
has done with these specific power points, and using, let's say,
people devoted to the living Avatar and other Avatars past who
have a similar calling related to the unity of religious ideas.

Certainly all of that, to me, is just a new, brilliant mechanism.
And I'm just lost in admiration that Meher Baba was suddenly
hit by his Whim and dreamed this one up on the spot,
apparently. I don't think this one was even known in God's latent
consciousness; I think this was Baba's total creativity (but let's not
get into that or we'll never get this book rolling at all). But at any
rate, here was that first snap. And I don't know how long I was
walking or standing just looking at this landscape that went on
forever ... it wasn't beautiful, but the power of it, the immensity
of it, it struck me terribly deeply. So then it just suddenly ended,
and suddenly I found myself at ... I never even speculated on

this, and where it came from I don't know and I still can't describe it, but I knew I was at the Om Point of the Creation.

WS: So this is after you kind of came back to...?

DES: I didn't even see where I was in between times … just one snapshot ended and a second snapshot started. I was totally immersed in the second snapshot. I didn't get a glimpse of what I was doing, where I was ....

WS: If you were moving or not, or ... ?

DES: I just went from one snapshot that I knew was a real glimpse of central important reality ...

WS: I didn't realize. So now you're in the second snapshot?

DES: Now, suddenly, I am in the second snapshot, and I know it is the birth [of the] Om Point.

April 10, 2010

Snapshot Two

DES: So here I was, the venue either London or Paris — a street, I don't know — and I was walking and suddenly the scene disappeared from my memory, totally disappeared and I was right in the middle of … all I can call it is a snapshot of Reality, because it had that impact and that association. I don't wonder, I don't have such types of visions; this is the only time in my life I've ever had this sort of an experience. It was absolutely unique and so definitive and so powerful that I didn't doubt any part of it, or even the intent of what was apparently being registered.

The first one is simply the realization of how vast infinitude actually is. I've studied infinity mathematics in the university. I've dealt with it at various times in mysticism, of course. And I realised instantly that this infinitely rolling on, ad infinitum landscape suddenly before me, that this was the closest thing visually that perhaps could be concocted to give, hopefully, know-it-all-neophyte Don Stevens a more clear idea of infinity. The closest I can describe it to is sort of a rolling, Midwestern USA prairie. There's no mountains, no rivers ... it just goes on sort of rolling. The details are not really details, but you realise that it's not a faceless landscape. It does have a face, and just as you have bumps and hollowings and so on in your own face, this had bumps and hollowings and so on. And it was all a sort of a nondescript, slightly greyish, light-tan color; there was nothing distinctive about the color.

WS: And a sky, Don?

DES: You know there was no division between landscape and sky. That was one of the extraordinary things about it; there was no hint of any separation. It was just all seamless, rolling, infinite landscape and it went on and on. And I knew that even if I could someway get a jet plane and travel, I would never see where it stopped, nor where it started, nor anything else about this infinitude. So infinite infinitude: it contains apparently endlessness and all-potentiality for any and all sorts of impressioned individuality to be made upon it. It's not insensitive, so it can be impressed. But there it was; it was not oppressive in the slightest bit. It didn't make me unhappy or pessimistic, not in the least little bit ... it had all-potentiality.

WS: Did you feel uplifted or ... ?

DES: No, it was just there. It just was, and the thing that was important was the enormity of what infinitude is. And I realized that before it was just sort of a mathematical concept to me, and I had no inner sense of how enormous infinitude is. It was just ... I knew it went on forever.

WS: And when you had this vision, Don, did you just stop still from walking, or did you have to lean against ... ?

DES: I just don't know what happened; I have absolutely no idea of what my body was doing. I was just absolutely bathed in this infinite landscape. And how I got there was not of interest to me; I knew that was a sidetrack.

WS: And you don't know what prompted it?

DES: No, it just suddenly was there, no antecedents at all. I couldn't say why this came, because in any reflecting I did later on, it was just astonishing that there were no antecedents to it, nothing I could relate. So I deliberately tried to see if there was something I had been doing which could have introduced even the subject [of infinitude] into my conscious mind and I couldn't think of having anything about infinitude crop through my mind for days and days and days. There was nothing alive which sparked it that I could see. It was just necessary for me to have an experience of the enormity of infinitude. And my God, it was just so incredible, no question about it, no astonishment about it, just … there it is. This is what, let's say, the base of God's reality is: just this incredible, impressionable, infinitude.

WS: So you knew then at the time, or later, that this vision had some significance for you, that it was important and necessary?

DES: There was no comparison with anything. It was just, I would say, the most complete single happening I've ever had in my life. It was all-complete; there was no room for speculation. Any bit of speculation or searching for this or that came later. But within the experience itself I wasn't surprised; I wasn't stunned; I wasn't overjoyed. It was just breathlessly, incredibly on, and on, and on, and on. It's just impossible to give a sense of the vastness of infinitude that was impressed on me in those few moments.

And then suddenly it was gone, and I was in another landscape. And in that particular landscape there was—as if it were, the base was the infinitude that I had experienced in the first snap—but there were things lying around on the surface of that rolling, rolling, rolling, greyish-tan landscape that just went on and on and on and on. And they were coiled, curled, locked, knotted and so on. There were separate ones; there was separation … there would be this one here, certain types of material it would seem, with a certain amount of complexity of looping and tying and so on.

And then over there would be another one of a slightly different colour consistency, and the manner in which it was looped and knotted and so on was distinct. And there was another one where apparently the original state of knotting and coiling had been handled, and some sort of simple order made out if it, usually just coiling it around like you would a garden hose. That was the only thing that ran through my mind associated with it: that some way, some of this mass of knots and coils and so on, all around all over this landscape, had been handled by the conscious will, [by] orderly mind, and that some knotting and looping and tangling had been removed from sections. And there were others which apparently had never been even touched at that point. But mostly, mostly, mostly some untangling, unknotting, unlooping had occurred and I just knew inside of myself this is the landscape of sanskaras.

WS: And did that remind you, like the first vision had reminded you, of the prairies of the Midwest? Did this remind you of any … ?

DES: No, that was only associated with the first snap. This had no associations that came into my mind. Definitely either it was in the first snap itself, or almost immediately after the snaps were done. That concept of the closest thing I ever saw to that was when I was out in the middle of the Midwestern prairies and they just went on and on, no farm houses around, no agricultural machines, nothing of the sort, just rolling landscape.

WS: And [in] this second vision you immediately knew that these were sanskaras?

DES: Yes, these were sanskaras. Some way or another I was tied internally into the reality of what they were. And it was certainly apparent that they were just incredibly there and just incredibly confused … confusing. And there was a great mass, just a huge mass, that obviously had been only just slightly straightened out, uncoiled, unknotted—just incredible. And I knew that this was, let's say, the in-between stage of God, of an important part of God. This was, let's say, not outside of God, but in some way I knew it was not integrated into the manifested latency of God. It was en route, but it was not yet reincorporated into the ultimate, eternal reality of infinitely, individualized consciousness of God. Does that make any sense?

WS: I think so, Don, yes.

DES: If it doesn't then we've got to go over it, because it's terribly important.

WS: So the first landscape related to that infinite, individualized consciousness?

DES: No, it was not individualized; it was just before anything had happened to that impressionable ...

WS: Yes, just infinite infinitude ...

DES: It was just, let's say, the original, original, original Beyond-Beyond state of God.

WS: Right. And then this second snapshot?

DES: Well, this was before the Whim ever manifested for no reason at all, as Baba impresses upon us. This was a state of virginity of God. But I knew that it was impressionable, that it could be handled and turned into any form, any shape, any identity ... any complexity. It was just simply waiting in abeyance and then, for no reason at all, the Whim moved. This was the pre-movement state of God.

WS: Latent?

DES: I was not even aware ... I knew it was impressionable, but don't ask me how. In other words it was not inert, [not] dead, but [rather] lacking anything to give form. So here we are then in the second state of impressionable God when, let's say, the landscape becomes cluttered up (and these were all on the surface; no part of any of these coiled things [was] buried into the impressionable mass of God). In other words this was, let's say, en route to manifestation and perfection, but not yet fused back into the infinite reality of God.

And of course this is a terribly important state. It's where most of what we are familiar with as Creation exists, in this sort of tangled up, messed-up state. And of course we are not aware of how tangled up and messed up these things are, because as far as the human being is concerned, all of these tangled masses and knotted masses are stored in the mental body. So they are not even susceptible to being consciously looked at and handled. It's only as they are awakened and, you might say, emerge from that mental body storehouse that some of the reality and the complexity — the challenge — begins to be revealed.

But here was, as if it were, a landscape un-reprieved from, let's say, the storehouse of the mental bodies. And of course I suppose many of them were simply in the very early, primitive states of the creation of the complexity of their sanskaric structure. I was not aware of that ... it's only now that I'm reflecting on it, all of the things that I saw in the landscape were pretty impressively coiled, knotted there. And when I think of it, certainly when the drop-soul has just emerged from the Om Point and does not even have any impressions yet associated with it, there can be nothing of that sort.

Now that of course goes back to the first snapshot. But then the second snapshot was pretty obviously at a fairly advanced stage of evolution — where there had been quite a bit of rebirths and new life-cycles going up the evolutionary scale — but the ones I saw were all pretty complex, and I didn't see any simple little forms which had apparently been formed in the early stages. Why they were absent, I don't know? I think because 'snap two' was preparatory to 'snap three.' Which is, let us say, the extraordinary complexity these things can get involved in within the infinitude of God being, let's say, everything experiencing everything.

So this, I would say, represented a sort of an eyeball contact with probably fairly advanced human-form sanskaras. And the complexity, and the differences of the complexities, were just sheerly incredible. I would never have dreamed that you could

get a cable or a garden hose, or anything, into all of the loops
and twists and turns and knots and tangles that these things
sitting around [had] — a pile here, a pile there, a pile there —
you know, just incredible.

WS: That's why we need the Avatar to help out, I suppose, to
straighten them?

DES: Well now, we haven't got to that point yet, so don't
jump the gun.

WS: No, sorry, Don. But you mentioned snap three. Did
that follow on immediately from snap two?

DES: Yes, after I had just been almost fatigued — mentally
fatigued, just seeing the complexity of all of these dammed
snarls and knots and so on lying around the landscape — I
mean, just immediately my mind leapt to: "What a God-awful
problem to try and get all of that mess straightened out into
some sort of decent, liveable ... at least coiled-up things that
don't happen to be knotted ... and taken out of the helpless
twists and turns that they're in." Because it just implied such
a tremendous amount of work to be done. For what reason, I
wasn't even speculating, but I just knew that this was the state
of fairly advanced human sanskaric structures.

WS: Complexity ...

Don Stevens (circa late 1970s). Place, date and photographer unknown.

Don Stevens with Kathryn Harris in Chicago, November 1978. (She had just met Don for the first time, thanks to Dick Duman). Photo by Susan Lutkendorf.

Don Stevens with Francis Brabazon at Meherazad, India (1980). Photo by Dick Duman. Copyright (c) 2014 by L. Weichberger.

Detail of Don Stevens at his London flat, 228 Hammersmith Grove, 1999 (with Lol Benbow and Keith Ashton). Photo copyright (c) 2014 by Lol Benbow. Used by permission.

Don Stevens with V.S. Bhau Kalchuri (June 2000). Place and photographer unknown.

Don Stevens hugging a Baba-lover in Atlanta, Georgia, 2007. Photograph by Doug Frank.

Don Stevens at the Avatar Meher Baba Center of Southern California, October 2007.
Photo by Douglas Frank

Don with the 2009 Beads on One String India Pilgrimage group, Mt. Abu, India, January,
2009. Photograph by Doug Frank.

Don Stevens with M. V. R. K. Balaji at the downtown Hyderabad Meher Baba Center, India, 2009. Photograph by Doug Frank.

Don with Sevn McAuley at the 40th Amartithi, Upper Meherabad, India, January 31, 2009.
Photo by Douglas Frank.

Snapshot Three

DES: Yes, right. So that was snap number two. And then we get into snap number three, and it was strange; I didn't see any faces, but I knew in the landscape that I was involved in — in snap three — that there were human forms, quite a few of them around that I had been familiar with in my own lifespan, in this lifetime. And I knew that here we were with that select body of people that I had got to know, quite a good many of them when they were actually alive — Baba's Mandali.

And as I saw them I knew that they housed within them sanskaric forms and patterns. But I knew, just as a part of the reality of the background (even though it was not visually before me), that in most of the human beings around me, with almost all of the twists and turns, quite a great mass of sanskaras had been straightened out — properly coiled, put into good order, into what should I say, proper, assimilable ... they could be assimilated into the permanent, infinite, individualized consciousness of God. Some of them, they were ready for that, but had not yet been — they were still housed in these individuals who I knew were Mandali.

And then I knew suddenly that the complexity of snap two — which was just simply overpowering by all the convolutions and knots and twists and so on that these things could get into — I knew just deeply and instinctively that there were a certain small proportion which [were] so complex and so tightly knotted, that it would just have been humanly impossible in space and time to uncoil them, unknot them, untwist them, and get them out into a free, assimilable state. So instantly I also knew that the rare situation where the human being, even after ... and this part I want to go into maybe in detail ad nauseam, because this to me was the thing that was so terribly important: that I knew that with some — the human beings who were there and I knew were Mandali — I knew that there was somewhere in each one of them a sanskaric knotting — a coiling and twisting — which had defied lifetimes and lifetimes of repeated effort. Sincere, deep, challenging effort. Not sort of weakened, "Ah, that's too complicated for me, I can't do this — you know" ... they were far past that sitting around, consoling and sympathizing with themselves. They had honest ... and I knew also that probably many of them had committed suicide several times — because they came to a total, total impasse in trying to get somewhere in this unknotting business, and finally just the sheer burden and the unmovableness of some of these complexities was just too much ... they couldn't stand it any longer.

And so there were, let's say, in humanity as it progressed, just statistically a certain — fortunately small residue — which surpassed even let's say the normally available knowledge of Truth that is available through the [Spiritual] Hierarchy, and through the residues that the Avatar keeps leaving. Even what was available was not enough to help them through it. And therefore they became just automatically ... because that's one of the things as to what the Avatar's all about, let's say, the things that demand the attention of the Master Mechanic of the whole system of what happens when the Whim starts moving. So "He" is the source of last resource.

"The general belief that suicide is bad is due to the fact that it is usually the result of low motives or a cowardly attitude towards life. When suicide is employed as an escape from dilemmas brought on by failure to cope with the needs of life, it is not only ignoble, but far reaching as well in its demoralizing effects upon the victim." — Meher Baba, in *Listen, Humanity* (p. 100) in "LH.pdf" downloaded from www.ambppct.org

WS: The last resort?

DES: The last resort to get this done. And I knew that he was very, very clever about this, and that is — I knew this even from things that Baba had hinted to me — that the very, very best way to get inside and do some handling and manipulating, is the Avatar. And of course the Avatar doesn't have to worry about knocking on the door and saying, "Please may I come in?" I mean he first of all gets the individual into a position of absolute trust, so he can make do with any part of the property of an individual drop-soul that he wants to without infringing, because he is so totally loved and trusted. So that's the first thing.

And then in order to make that state really usable, his ploy — and it's a deliberate thing that he does, you know — Baba says, "You think that I need your help, but I don't need your help. I can get all of these things done, but I let you help me — to help you." And this explains

Don Stevens made it a point to tell us that in the past, in Baba's dealings with him, that Baba waited to be "invited in" to any aspect of Don's life before working with him on that area. - LCW

exactly what is going on there, because that distracts their ego attention. And the ego — when it is distracted from what it is doing, what it is involved in — things can happen to the energy patterns which couldn't happen if the ego were around bossing the thing. The ego would in some way rearrange the thing at the end of the day, for the ego had its way and felt satisfied, and it "winds up" some new counter-sanskaras again.

But if the ego is completely, as it were, anesthetized and refocused somewhere else — and does things just almost mechanically that it forgot [needed] to be done — [then] the presence of the Avatar, and the bewitchment of working for the Avatar (with all of this love and bliss that you feel when you're in a fling with the Avatar) has swept your ego into a state

For more about the winding and unwinding of sanskaras in a human being see Meher Baba, *Discourses*, Volume I, p. 61, "The Formation and Function of Sanskaras", and also: Volume I, p. 66. "The Removal of Sanskaras." at discoursesbymeherbaba.org

of total mismanagement of ego desires. You see what's going on? This is a clever ploy: using the Avatar's own work as the ultimate distraction. It's incredible.

WS: And then the work is done "through the back door," in a sense, while the ego is over there …

DES: The ego is not even aware of what's going on.

WS: So do you think this is how these drop-souls — the Mandali — are helped by the Avatar?

DES: Yes, the Avatar takes them into some part of his work that he knows is harmonious with the pattern of that particular drop-soul, that's ideally suited for them, to really capture their imagination and their desire to help.

WS: So this was snap three?

DES: This was snap three. Now the thing that is terribly important here for me, and I want to be sure registers, is what this did (and here I've got to risk

For what Meher Baba said about his own work with his Mandali, or Circle, see: *Discourses*, Volume III, p. 44, "The Circle." - LCW

being overly personal, overly honest). I've had several people in my life — almost in all cases people that I got to know after I had met Baba face-to-face, and Baba put me in touch with — whom I regarded as ... not even next door to Perfection, but just, you know, a gossamer-curtain away from Perfection. And then all of sudden [to] see them do unexpectedly something that would seem so terribly primitive and naïve and thoughtless and even cruel? And I said [to myself], "My God, I would never have dreamed that this human being who I would swear is a gossamer curtain away ... how could they do anything that is so blatantly different and unworked out — just as if it was in the original caveman days of primitive, you know, destructiveness?" Does this make sense?

WS: Yes. Did you see this with most of the Mandali that you had dealings with — that occasionally there would be this totally...

DES: It was not necessary for me to see it in all Mandali. Let's say just a glimpse of it in two (or three, or four), or maybe five of my favorite-favorite-favorite Mandali.

WS: So every now and then something would shock you in their behavior, or in what they said or did?

DES: Yes. And then I would say to myself, "Well, I guess that's why they are still even Mandali, but obviously not yet perfected." And somewhere there is a knot, and this is the evidence of the knot coming out here ... It's real, they would act just like a primitive human being with this knot of sanskaras. And when I knew this inside of myself — that this is why they became the

technical responsibility of the Master Mechanic of Creation —
that automatically this is one of the duties of the Avatar, to handle
those extraordinarily important … Now, quite frankly, it was also
evident to me the amount of tough, tough effort that each of these
individuals had put into trying. It was a tremendously chastening
thing. And so it was like, let's say, having a bar of steel that you're
turning into a rapier [sword] with a sharp edge — and the amount
of re-forging and re-forging that this particular bar of steel had
gone through produced just some incredible qualities of spring
and, you know, just almost superhuman beings, just super beings.

   That's why the Mandali are, almost without an exception, such
super persons. And yet there's that one hang-up that had to go to
the Avatar's desk to get straightened out. But they are sincerely,
actually, functioning as practically superhuman beings, and the
strength of some of their qualities are just breathtaking, because
they just seem so superhuman. And that's for real. But I had always
looked on it as being, let's say, an important fact of imperfection,
and wondered how under the sun I could in some way or another
one day describe even the Mandali in terms that were not
condemning? And when I saw this — that they were the super
product — that they are, because of the trials and tribulations, and
the knowing that they just could not give in … Even when they
would commit suicide, they knew that it was not the end. It was
just a temporary lull that they had to have, some way or another, to
recoup their forces to go back.

   So these incredible qualities of the Mandali are there. And
the fact that each one has a knot which [has] to be untied by the
Avatar himself does not diminish the quality or the reality and the
wonderfulness of these superb qualities which had been forged by
honest, repeated, insistent effort to do the unsnarling that had to
be done on this one particular thing that resisted. But the other
sanskaras are all done.

   WS: Do you think being so close to the Avatar — and as you
say the gossamer veil is so thin for the Mandali — that the really

primitive sanskaras have to come up, because they're the last ones that would have to be unknotted?

DES: I would even hesitate to even put sanskaras in the plural. I think there is one ... I think it would be terribly unusual to have even two knots like that.

WS: And do you think for each of the Mandali there was a different knot, a different final sanskara?

DES: Oh yes, depending on the particular, original personality — because certainly having dealt with that sanskara

Please note that this idea that there is one sanskaric knot left in each one of the Mandali is a Don-ism, and not directly reflected in the Meher Baba literature. Eruch Jessawala did admit to being a "glutton" before coming to live with Baba, so there is some circumstantial evidence to support what Don is saying. - LCW

after lifetimes and lifetimes and lifetimes, there's certainly a very strong personality which is created in the process. So they do have terribly strong personalities, there's no question about it.

WS: So that being with the Avatar, and doing the work of the Avatar in such a devoted and loving way, they're also being helped to unravel this really fundamental knot that's there?

DES: It is, let's say, the Avatar's unique way of doing it, and I feel that only the Avatar could do it that way. I think that is the way he has set up Creation. So in other words only the Avatar ... {interrupted when the doorbell rings on the 228 Hammersmith Grove flat.}

DES: ....Why this snap three was so important to me, because to be perfectly honest I've known that certainly I would have to sit down and record words about, let's say, these experiences of Don Stevens with even several of my closest, closest, most deeply admired Mandali. And I dreaded how under the sun am I going to put this into words, because it sounds as if they have a side to them like some caveman resuscitated ... somebody at the door? {They take a break to answer the door...}

DES: .... I have a dread, and this is a terrible thing to live with because, you know, people I love ... I really love them, and I don't know if my love has to deal only with perfection. I don't think that it does, because even after my favorites would do something that would shock the living daylights out of me, I still loved them as much … In fact I loved them even more. And just the idea [that] one day I know I'm going to have to put this into words, and they're going to have to be public words. And how can I bear to do it, because it seems to me like a betrayal of this deep feeling that I have, especially for the close, close, close Mandali, who are the closest people to me I've ever had, except for Baba himself.

So this was a major, major problem. And when I saw snap three, and saw that the Mandali are these special cases for the Avatar, and that somewhere there was a knot that resisted superhuman efforts, and that it demanded the direct intercession of the Avatar, I knew that I could point this out. Because you know having one particular flaw makes sense after all. You keep getting born until all the sanskaric mess is cleaned up, and you even have to go through a final inspection by a Perfect One, as Baba says, before you get though the pearly gates and are taken into that situation of Infinite, Eternal Oneness with God. So that's very special.

So the very fact that they're here as human beings implies there's still something that is not quite sorted out. And I knew also that at the same time that here was the explanation of why they all have just unquestionably, just superhuman qualities which had been forged into their nature. And when I realized this I said, "Oh my God, I can write this as a bouquet of flowers or a crown of diamonds for each one with what I realize now," because it explains the beauty and the magnificence of the nature that these people do have. So I don't need to worry.

Honesty

May 1, 2010

*D*on: I want to pick up, not where we left off because I'm sure I can't remember, but as I recall a recording stint came to an end when I had started a very, very, vivid chapter in my relationship with Baba. And that was the manner in which I became involved directly[with] him in two vows of honesty that I realised, soon after he dropped the body, had been one of the most productive and important things that had ever happened to me in my relationship with Baba. And because it happened so unconsciously, it struck me all in a heap when I realised it. So I'll pick up and assume that I gave the beginning background for those two.

One had to do with the Sufis who were coming in under Baba's direction and were taking a vow to the Murshida. And included in that [was] of course material that Baba had put together, but that Murshida Duce, Lud Dimpfl and I contributed to also. So there was as a vow of absolute honesty that had just raised literal hell with Sufi members, and husbands said, 'I'll get divorced by my wife if I'm honest, and my family will disown me, and my boss will fire me.' And the wife of course had similar woes.

So Baba said, "Well, this is important. When I get to America finally to meet my new Sufi brethren, then I will go into what Baba means by absolute honesty."

And the other situation in which he got me involved ... he crept up rather cautiously into whether I was absolutely honest in my business dealings. Because he knew, as many people knew, that especially big petroleum was supposed to be big corruption and all sorts of things were reputed to go on (I'm afraid many of which were perfectly true, and a lot of people made dishonest fortunes). But finally it came to just the blunt question from Baba one day,

'Don, are you allowed to be absolutely honest?' And I assured him that I was not only allowed to be, but strangely enough my management insisted that I be. I think that was when I began to realize that the company I was working for was an incredible example of total honesty enforced from the highest level.

And so when Baba dropped his body, it was just as if a veil had been removed from the conscious and unconscious level, and I realised how tremendously important this had become unwittingly on my part through the course of years in two fields (and [in] both of those fields just terribly central). First of all: actually in working out a mechanism by which I became gradually conscious of the unexpected manners in which one's own personal sanskaras entered into the basic energizing and motivating patterns of one's action. And where I would not have realized when I began this whole business of checking on my honesty (because I vowed twice to Baba that I would be), I saw that in the course of time it was sort of like the old onion with layers and layers and layers that we talk about with various things, especially on the spiritual path. There are just layers and layers and layers to them, and honesty is one of those. And one sees that an awful lot of rationalization, unconscious mostly, and kidding oneself, almost totally unconscious, goes on. And it's only when you have some particularly deeply meaningful need to pursue the depth of your honesty or dishonesty in your daily life that you begin to see just all of the prevaricating ... is that a good word?

WS: I think so, Don.

DES: For some reason it just doesn't sound quite right, that's why I hesitated on it. Anyway I can't use "lying," because certainly nobody would admit to lying to oneself. But you know, white lies or fibs or something ... how much of all of this goes on in our lives. It's only under some sort of conscious prod.

It is a great word! Prevaricate: to deviate from the truth. - LCW

{Phone rings ... they take a short break.}

DES: This became terribly important in two fields [where] I saw about just how much had gone on. One is to pierce underneath and reveal to me more and more the manner in which our stored sanskaras, without our realizing what's going on, influence very deeply and centrally our activities — decisions that we take, how we conduct ourselves. And it's a pretty murky field that gradually emerges.

And also I became aware of the fact — I'm convinced of this … I don't know how this works, but when one, let's say, builds a conscious tunnel into the inner workings of motivation in one's personal life, somewhere or another I'm convinced that helps the process of wearing down and getting rid of the sanskaras. I don't want to say that it's the only way that they're worn down. I'm just sure if one follows through daily life and keeps trying to do one's best, and keeps making decisions and acting, there is a gradual balancing that does occur.

But I'm just dead convinced that when one begins to get onto the trail of the sneakiness — the unexpectedness of how these things happen in our daily life without our realizing it — somewhere or another when the bird is out there and exposed to light, by golly he can be evicted from his nest, I'm pretty sure, a lot faster in our lives. So I just feel that the vow of honesty to oneself, or to Baba or whatever is meaningful in one's life, can be of immeasurable help with one's own personal sanskaras. Baba never discussed this with me, but I am sure that is part of why he insisted on it. And it is in the vows Sufism Reoriented took and new Sufis take to this day, presumably.

Now the other field where it was unexpected: I realised that for years and years and years it had become an automatic habit, even without my realizing it, that there was not even a medium important decision that I took during the course of the day when I did not just quickly bring that up to my inner life, my inner judgement, and say, "Don, as far as you know would acting in the manner you're thinking of doing it correspond to honest action that Baba has asked? Are you able to do this, and are you pretty sure that this is consistent with it?" So that does two things: first of all it brings something to bear. And secondly, without even trying to, it just naturally, normally, brings Baba right into your daily life. You don't have to remember he's right there, because you promised it. And you can't go through this action meaningfully without, you know, just … he's there! And I never questioned it. Baba had made it terribly evident to me that he was always around … life was completely transparent.

But he did not, let's say, intrude into my life (and certainly not in an important way) without some way or another checking as to whether I was inviting him into that situation. This was one of the strange graces especially of the Avatar: he never got inside the door without being invited.

WS: Was this [the] same before and after Baba dropped the body, or was there a change there?

DES: No, absolutely. Well, after all you remember my story of my twenty-four hours getting to Baba and all of the "Iranis." And finally when I got into that line for the Poona flight, the guy next to me said, "My name is Irani" as they were writing down the people present, and I just shouted out loud, "Baba, you don't

This story is about Don's journey to the Last Darshan - the entombment of Avatar Meher Baba at Meherabad, February 1969. - LCW

have to keep repeating this, I got it now!" {Don and Wayne laugh … } And they all looked at me as if I was crazy. There I was, just shouting out a crazy thing into mid-air. And so Baba, you know, got his drilling home to me: "The fact that I had dropped My physical body has nothing to do with our relatedness and our closeness, and how I function in relation to you. I'm here!"

This is a case of Don paraphrasing what he feels Baba said to him intuitively after dropping his physical form. - LCW

WS: Has that increased, do you think, that sense of Baba's presence?

DES: Well, do you remember once — I'm sure I've told you this story, but it bears repeating. I became aware once when I was

telling the story about Meherjee Karkaria talking to the group in
Marseille, and some dear little old lady in the group at the time
said, "Meherjee, how under the sun can you bear the pain of
separation from Baba, because you were so close to him, and had
immediate access to him we all know, and now he's not around any
longer?"

And Meherjee, you know, just looked at her as if she had said
probably the craziest thing he'd ever heard and said, "Listen, no,
not at all, when he was actually in the body and I was traveling, he
was over there in India, but now he's with me all of the time." In
fact he said, "He's over my right shoulder. I'm sure if I look around
that I will see him there, actually!"

And that was exactly the sensation that I had, but had never
told anybody, and to hear Meherjee say that's where he is … God,
I said, "Stevens, you're not nuts after all!" And so that was a great,
great finding.

And then, when I was telling that story on one occasion, I
suddenly thought I'm being dishonest, because I hadn't had that
sense that he's just over and back of my right shoulder for some
time now. And I felt so … as if the world had caved out from
underneath me and that I just lost something, and it was probably
due to negligence somewhere or another on my part … nxious
to blame myself of course. But then immediately this little wispy
voice inside of me cropped up, the [same] one that said, "Don,
why don't you make friends with your body, instead of being mad
at it?" The same little voice, you know, that every once in a while
would come in very unexpectedly. And it said, "Don, it's because
he's in you now, no longer over the shoulder, [but] inside of you … "

WS: No longer over the shoulder, but?

DES: Inside, yes, even more intimately involved. But at any
rate, here was something that I realized had been invaluable: that
automatically by checking my sense of what would Baba consider
as being a honest business action, without it being a law that he
had laid down to me. Check with Baba — I did it automatically

and that had been going on for decades (well, not decades and decades, but quite a few years when Baba had dropped the body). And I realized, by golly, probably [between] that and the translation work which I checked for Baba — which became just very hot and heavy for quite a long time — Baba was just very consciously in my mind. And so between those two things ... but the vow of honesty was an automatic one, and boy, it was frequent. So I was just checking with Baba through an inner sense, as it were, his sense of honesty — what would work, and what is dishonest.

WS: And that ties in with conscience as well, does it, Don, do you think? It's all part of the same mechanism and inner structure ... a person's conscience?

DES: Well, to be perfectly honest I've never really known what conscience was, because it never seemed to function the way I'd understand it from conversations, because I'd been so reared by my mother to be absolutely honest in all relationships, you know. Not just with money, but everywhere along the line, because most people bring up conscience in relation to money and honesty, yes. But it was just there, and so I never checked against my conscience.

WS: It sounds like you had a good grounding in honesty before you came to Baba?

DES: Yes, it was an automatic principle. And so I did not apparently have, let's say, a streak of dishonesty which needed correction and [for which] I had to bring some sort of truing, internal Don Stevens guide into it, which is what I would have interpreted conscience to be. It wasn't needed. It wasn't there ... There was nothing to be done. But when Baba got his nose into it from a business standpoint, then I had to think — Well, Baba's got some pretty strict standards, and I just thought I'd better be sure I check this for that order, that this is proper and smells right.

So those were the two things that I wanted to bring out, especially in relation to the two vows of honesty to Baba. That it was paramount in those two important facts: remembering Baba, not as command, but just by an automatic reflex. And also as a deep, deeper way to go deeper into the manner in which our stored sanskaras get tangled up in situations. And when one really gets down and pries through the onion skin layers, and gets to the heart of the thing finally, and knows just how deeply these things do affect us, then that some way or another speeds up. I just know it in my bones — the process of balancing them out and wearing out the compulsive energy — it's just enormously ... In fact, I think it deals a deathblow to that particular sanskara's compulsive energy when we just finally realize how deep it had gone. That you had to make an absolute decision not to allow it, if it was contrary to your own feeling of happy living ... Just that simple.

WS: Which is, I suppose, also coming closer to God for people on the spiritual path?

DES: Well, I've never had too much of a relation with God. {Laughs} I mean as far as I was concerned, He was always something that sat off on the mountain somewhere or another and was probably very important, but had absolutely no practical significance in my life. And of course when I met Meher Baba, I just knew that this was, let's say, the essence of God regardless. And there he was ... he was my buddy! You can't get much closer than that. And I was just certain that he accepted me and that we had a terribly good, working, safe relationship.

Meher Baba and Finances

May 1, 2010

*D*on: The other subject that I want to start getting into is Meher Baba and money. This came up first of all in relation to, oddly enough, the fact that Meher Baba had been planning a Four Language Groups Sahavas, [in India] especially with young Baba followers. And when I had a kidney infection and could not accept his invitation to Baba men devotees from the West, he sent me word, "Don't worry, Don, I'll make it up to you." And then when he was planning this Four Language Groups Sahavas, he invited me and Francis Brabazon as the only Westerners. So that was absolutely wonderful. And as soon as I got there, I was put up in the upper quarters over the old water tank on Meherabad Hill, where the Samadhi is.

And then it was the following morning when I went down to the central Mandali Hall [at Lower Meherabad], where Baba was going to be holding the Four Language Groups seminars. Baba was not yet there when I came. And when his car drove up, he just very, very quickly nodded his head at everybody and reached over to me, pulled on my sleeve and said, "Don, come with me. I've got to tell you something." Now, I don't even remember who translated that, but I was certainly not aware of any translating. And I do not know how under the sun he took me to [this] little shack home.

So there we were, it was empty, no question about that, and somebody must have been there translating [Baba's

The first invitation Don refers to from Baba was to Western men only, which later became known as the Three Incredible Weeks Sahavas. - LCW

Don remembered that shack as the one which was later occupied by Ted and Janet Judson for years until they built a new house, near the new archives building.

gestures], but I was oblivious of anybody else being there except
Baba. And Baba said, "Don, I just had to tell you immediately how
this language group was planned." Now this completely
flabbergasted me. Why should Baba feel he had any right to tell me
how he planned it?

And here he was, he didn't even take time to address a lot of these people that he had known ever since they were babies who were coming to the place, and there were a few older people involved in the

The editors felt Don meant "Why did Baba feel I had the right to hear how he planned it?" but we left the original words from Don.

arrangements. He did not embrace even a single person before he
dragged me off to the Judson's shack and said, "I've got to tell you
about this." So he said, "I have had a bank account with," — I
think it was 10,000 rupees — that was a pretty sizable sum of
money. And so he said, "I've decided to use that." Now he did not
say what he hoped to accomplish. He didn't bother with those
really esoterically important things that it was aimed at, but he just
went right to the bare bones of financing — I had a bank account
and it was that amount of money. So he said that when he saw the
exact figure, he then sent word to [Pendu] that he wanted to talk
over some arrangements for a meeting.

So [Pendu] comes, and Baba puts to him what he's going to do. [Baba's] going to have one week for each language group, so over four weeks each language group is handled separately. And he had I think it was somewhere around twenty [more]

In *Listen, Humanity* it is Pendu who is in charge of finances for the Sahavas (p.p. 32-34). While Don thought it was Padri, the editors are sure he meant Pendu.

people that he wanted to invite. He said he thought he didn't ever
want it just to be [an open] free invitation. He said the place would
have been drowned [with people], and he wanted it on a pretty
carefully chosen basis. So that he had then warned all of the heads
of the groups in India that he would issue an invitation through
them, through the group head, to these people that he wanted to
come. And under no circumstances were they to let it get around

what was going on, or that they were not being invited, because this was only a pretty small proportion of the total number of eligible young people, of course.

So [Baba] said that when he said how many people he wanted for how long, [Pendu] was just aghast, and said, "Baba, I don't think there's enough money for that?" And so Baba said he had to spend several hours with [Pendu] going over his ideas of the things that should be provided and narrowing them down to what [Baba] felt would be not threadbare provision, but nevertheless certainly not luxurious provisions.

And so [Baba] said, "After quite a long time of our comparing our ideas of what was necessary and what was not, then finally [Pendu] agreed that for the ten thousand rupees he could provide the necessary lodging." ... to rent beds, for instance, things of that sort, and of course food is a pretty big item.

So when all of this had been worked out, [Pendu] finally said, "Okay, let's do it."

And then of course immediately the news did get out to those who weren't supposed to know about it, and who were not being invited, and of course they raised all sorts of hell with the local group heads: ... "Why wasn't I invited?" etc., etc.

So Baba said he was just bombarded through Adi Sr. with additional people who wanted to come, and he said — I just had to be hard-hearted and just tell them no, unfortunately no, and not explain myself, not ask for forgiveness or anything, but just say no.

In cases where the editor felt Don was paraphrasing Baba, we decided not to use direct quotation marks. - LCW

And that's the first time I ever saw Baba in that sort of a position of some way or another implying that there [is] the esoteric aristocracy, and there are others who don't meet certain requirements for certain special occasions in Baba's mind. So that was a bit of an eye-opener for me, but he insisted on that absolutely; [he] made no compromise.

WS: So Baba chose who was going to be there?

DES: Yes, it was his [choice or decision and] he did not take recommendations from group heads or anyone of the sort, he told the group heads whom he wanted. I think in most instances he carefully consulted group heads on all sorts of things. Baba didn't run a dictatorship by any means. He really did a lot of sounding out, but on certain things he would make the decision, even at the beginning, and just stick to it … What sort of criterion applied there, he never did explain. It was just typical of the way Baba operated. There were certain principles. He didn't sit around and waste his time and your time explaining why it was that way.

WS: He told you just what he thought you needed to know?

DES: Just what was necessary to get the show on the road, and sometimes not [even] that. As you know about those motion pictures that he had me take, after all he sure waited that one out. And so then finally when he had spent … oh, I think he took at least half an hour explaining how carefully he'd gone over all of this, how the people were selected and so on … and then he said, "Well, we'd better go back." So everybody was waiting in Mandali Hall when Baba and I and somebody emerged from [the] shack and came over. And so I sat down way back over near the opening door, and Baba was raised up about in the centre of the room, and there were people clustered around. There were more than twenty-five; I assure you of that.

The motion pictures Don mentioned are films of Baba, and special places that Baba asked Don to film all around India, which Don took in the 1960s.

And Baba, when he was telling me this story, said that news did get out, and various group heads came to him with all sorts of tales of woe: … "Baba, we have this very fine person and he's not invited, and it's breaking his heart."

Baba said — Of course these came in, and some of them I just couldn't say no to, so I had to have a second conference with Pendu. And when Pendu found out how many additional people I wanted to add on, he threw up his hands in horror, and it took me practically all day to get that one straightened out. {Laughter}

But you see how careful Baba was. Pendu was the arrangement-walla, and Baba absolutely felt — I've got to have his okay – I'm not going to go over his head and say it's got to be done. Baba didn't work that way. This was really, to me, incredible.

So we're sitting there, and Baba is going into his song and dance, and his words are being translated from gestures into … I can't remember, I think it was maybe Marathi … anyway, translated into the proper language. And all of a sudden everybody sits bolt upright because there's a screech of brakes outside of the Mandali Hall window. And it sounded as if there was going to be an accident or a loud piercing scream, [like] somebody had just gotten killed or mortally wounded. It was obvious that a car was braking in an emergency fashion. And so Baba wiggled his fingers, and somebody back by the door goes outside and comes back in, and Baba has a wiggled conversation with that person and just does that to it. And we don't know what's going on. And so then all goes on with those original … I guess it's about forty people who the twenty-five had grown to with Baba's permission originally, but all this business of the screeching brakes, nobody knows until lunchtime.

So just as I'm finishing lunch, Baba sends word [that] he wants me. We go back over to [the] shack again, and he said — Don, you can't imagine what happened … you heard those brakes going on?

And I said, "Yes, was there an accident, Baba?"

And [Baba] said — No, it's just that there were these five young boys who had been sitting around late the previous day and bemoaning the fact that none of them had gotten an invitation. And one of them simply said, look, we've got a car. What do you think would happen if we got in the car and drove there and said hello? What do you think would happen? And the other four were just aghast at such an insurrection in the ranks, but the more they thought about it, they thought why not? The worse that could happen is [Baba would] say get out of here and go back home. At least we may have seen Baba, maybe even said hello to him, maybe even had an embrace. We can't lose anything.

And so they decided to come, and [Baba] said that was the five boys who came. And he said — Don, you cannot imagine. I've spent my entire lunchtime with Pendu, saying Pendu is there any way we can take these five boys in? And when Pendu heard that he just went through the roof. He just said, Baba, you squeezed me and squeezed me and squeezed me, but we're still managing to do it, and I think things are acceptable. But five more after that further increase of fifteen or so ... it's too much Baba. And Baba said well, you know what, I'll tell you what I can do, Padri. I can bring up some almost completely unknown spiritual truths which will be so fascinating that nobody will think about what food they're eating ... {Don and Wayne both laughing}

WS: Yes!

DES: ... and we can do still a healthy diet, but not maybe quite as appetizing as we had been planning on. And he said that — When I explained that to Pendu, [he] burst out laughing and said, "Oh Baba, you're impossible. It'll work, it'll work!" So, Pendu finally accepted it, but I had told the five boys they can come.

WS: Compassion.

DES: Compassion, yes, compassion. But don't count on it! — that was the moral of that story. It's pretty dangerous territory.

WS: Yes.

DES: So Baba showed me what he meant about how Baba handles finances. He said — Don, I wanted you to know how Baba handles an important public event where quite a good bit of money has to be spent. And it is all worked out carefully to the last paisa (or whatever it is), and it's worked out usually with Pendu, because he's the one. But always, always the money is there. It's not borrowed. It's not put onto a mortgage, or something like that. The money is there. It is available, and then it's worked out carefully exactly what could be covered and how. So that was the manner in which Baba showed me about public events.

Then after I had been going back and forth for a couple of years, I was actually sleeping in the Blue Bus most of the time and seeing just what a terribly simple life the Mandali who lived directly with Baba lived. And I thought, here's Stevens going to all of these posh hotels, going to great restaurants and entertaining all of these petroleum people. And I just thought, "God, I just can't think of doing that when Baba and his wonderful Mandali are living this sort of life." And I just thought, "I'm going to have to go back to the university and take some courses in Social Welfare, and get into something that's closer to the good of humanity than even petroleum is."

So that all got finally thrashed out, and then I said, "Baba, I've had this project of mine for a long time, wanting to give you from my monthly salary a certain amount of money."

Baba looked sort of interested and impressed, and he said, "Oh Don, what made you think of that?"

And I said, "Baba I can't bear this business of seeing the simple life that you and the Mandali lead, and I lead that plush life in petroleum."

So he said, "How much do you want to give me?"

And I said, something like — I would like to give you $500 a month — Which was a big chunk of money from a monthly cheque at that time.

And he looked a little amazed and shocked, and said, "Don, that's quite a good bit. I'm sure it's a large proportion of your salary?"

And I said, "Well, it's a pretty good chunk, but I live simply, Baba." And he whittled and he whittled and he whittled, and then we got it down to $200. And then he felt satisfied that we'd whittled enough there.

And then he began to say, "Well Don, what about your mother? After all she's a widow."

And I said, "Yes, but she remarried and her husband doesn't get a big salary, but … "

He went all through all of my relations — brothers, the [sisters-in-law], he wanted to know this, and he wanted to know that. "Now what happens if you suddenly get sick?" He went into just about everything …

WS: The details.

DES: … absolute, total details. None of this flashing —I'm the Avatar, and I know everything — sort of thing. He just wanted to know in practical, living life terms, here and now, what the propositions are. So can you imagine he would not agree to that $200 for … I think it was almost a year of visits back and forth, and each time I would bring it up again with him. And we would go into some more checking this and checking that … And [he said] — Don, what if I say for a time there's a project going on that so and so … or maybe one of my Mandali is in dire straits and I say, Don, for six months (or a year or so) give it to such and such a person who you already know? And what happens if you don't particularly like the person I want to give it to, what do you do then? You see the meticulous manner in which he went about this thing? And it took all of that length of time — almost a solid year — just spending all sorts of Avataric time on that! Can you imagine … I was flabbergasted. I could just not believe it.

September 24, 2010

DES: There are, of course, other things that came up during those conversations between Baba, Eruch, and myself that would be interspersed between the work that we were doing on editing. ... I would usually arrive for my visits with Baba with Meherjee Karkaria. Meherjee would have picked me up from the airport in Bombay and then driven me up as far as Poona, where I would spend the night. And then we would be quickly whisked over by his driver to Ahmednagar and Meherazad, usually to be with Baba fairly early the following morning. So Meherjee was a pretty constant theme. And as most people know, Meherjee was primarily a businessman, during the latter part of his career he was the founder and the head of the very specialized filter paper that was used in a good deal of very fine industrial establishments, such as beer and liquor manufacturers and so on. And of course they have to be doubly careful that anything introduced into the production system is top quality.

So the fact that Meherjee put out the highly reputed, trusted filter papers for much of the industry (I don't know how many of even Baba devotees [knew this] ... I think most people knew it had something to do with filter papers) – but it was this top, top grade that Meherjee had captured which was so important. And because of the fact that Meherjee was right there, Baba would usually take the occasion to have a private conversation with [him] before Meherjee would be leaving to go back to Poona, after having delivered me. But the thing that surprised me was that when Baba was having his private conversation with Meherjee, almost always he would – this just amazed me – he would ask Eruch to leave, and he did not ask me to leave. He kept me in on his conversations with Meherjee.

WS: There were just the three of you?

DES: Yes. Baba, Meherjee and myself.

WS: Who would interpret Baba then, or would Meherjee understand?

DES: Oh, Meherjee would interpret what I couldn't pick up. And so that was the basis on which I found out two things: the first one was that, as far as finances were concerned, Baba trusted Meherjee, and his judgment, as he trusted nobody else's. That was an amazing fact. And secondly it gave me the opportunity to see Baba's functioning as a financial wizard, and boy he was fast and sharp. I, of course, being in the bulk crude-oil sales for so long, where just huge sums of money are involved (and if you make a mistake on a barrel of a quarter of a cent, you know it piles up into a few million dollars pretty darn fast) and so, not because I was a mathematical genius, or a financial genius, but because my sales involved such colossal amounts of money, I was constantly around people who were really expert in the financial field. So I knew the financial department of Chevron intimately as if they were, let's say, my own department. And also I knew the chief financial officers of a good many of the principal petroleum companies of the world. So I had a fairly good background of [appraisal] to compare the conversations between Baba and Meherjee. And I knew what was considered [to be] a top financial wizard in finances, and certainly Meherjee was tops – no question about it. And Baba's command of the financial realities, and what could be done – and what must not be done, was just absolutely, completely, spot on.

WS: In what way, Don, would [Baba] understand the workings … ?

DES: Well, you know, exchange rates, and what exchange rates are probably going to go up and what are going to go down. It was principally, let's say, foreign exchange where Meherjee would get involved. And of course that was where I had most of my experience of him, for Baba had lots of donations coming in from abroad, people living abroad and telling Baba that they wanted to donate some money to him. So financial dealings with Meherjee usually involved exchanges of money almost automatically, and Meherjee was terribly good at it.

So I think one of the very first things that Baba did as an aside to me (and Meherjee just had to wait while Baba got done explaining this to me), he said, "Don, you may think from these conversations that Baba is wealthy with all of these people wanting to give him money, but let me assure you Baba almost never accepts a donation, because he knows the motives in back of most wishes to give money. And Baba knows that the person is expecting to get something back from Baba for the money that he is passing over and, of course, I can't accept it on that base. And so it is a rare occasion when I have … " He simply said, "[I] have had people promise me millions of dollars … " or pounds or whatever not, " … and, even though I might be very hard-up at that point, I could not accept the promise for such a gift, and I would find an excuse for not accepting it, thank the person for their kind thoughts … " and so on.

So Baba made that just terribly clear to me. And I knew, of course, when he said that, that had to be true, for I was around enough at the time. For instance, people like Elizabeth Patterson and Norina Matchabelli who practically … Norina, I guess, gave away one or two small fortunes. Elizabeth, of course, had the family foundation [in] back of her … she certainly turned an awful lot of money over to Baba. So they, and Meherjee himself … and there were one or two of the Mandali that Baba would accept very large gifts from.

WS: I get the impression that most gifts, or offers of donations, Baba had to … ?

DES: They were turned down, most of them were turned down. Smaller gifts, let's say, were usually offered with a clean bill of health. In other words, just given with a good deal of love. But the great big ones were … Baba wanted it made quite clear that almost without exception they were always turned down. And that there were certain long-term devotees who were fairly well-to-do that Baba would accept money from when he needed it. So Baba [repeatedly] said, of course, "I often turn my pockets inside out to show people there is nothing in them." And he said, "It is true that I very rarely deal with finances because the manner of receiving them, [and] the projects that they're to be expended on, are so well known. And when a new project comes up, we always discuss carefully how it is to be handled ... " and so on.

So actually it is fairly rare that Baba even discusses money. But the thing that I want to clarify was the one occasion when, for whatever reason, Baba felt that he wanted to give me a basic education in how carefully he sought the financing of especially his major projects with groups of Baba devotees. And this occurred when he invited Francis Brabazon and me to come to what was called the Four Language Groups Sahavas in the early 1950s ...

But can you imagine postponing the whole group for half an hour in order to explain to me the final [financial] chapter? So this gives to you an idea the care to finances that Baba took, contrary to all stories. Even the closest Mandali said, "Baba never talks about money ... We know Baba's going to provide, but how he provides, you know, it's a gift from him."

It isn't a gift from him! He took me right down into the middle of basic planning of one of the most important meetings he had given, and took me through the critical steps that [go] on. I couldn't believe it! And I was just – so proud of our Avatar – for how he goes about it, and the care and the skin-flinting ... even my Swedish mother can't save like Baba could figure it out!

So finally, between the sessions with Meherjee and Baba's insistence on telling me that, I found out that Baba was terribly careful about money. And this business about Baba never talking about money or handling money or discussing money, is on the surface true. But nevertheless the reality is, I don't think there is a treasurer of any corporation anywhere in the world who handles finances as carefully and as thoughtfully and as totally, totally honestly, ethically, as Baba does ... This is an eye-opener.

WS: Do you think there were any messages there, Don, that

were meant for the future in relation to ... ?

DES: Just that all of this talk which comes primarily from even the closest of the Mandali, it is a deliberate veneer that Baba has papered over, because money is not important. It is necessary and an important vehicle, but it is not one of the things that really counts – but you've got to be careful with it. It's just like the body. The body – you are going to get rid of it finally, and it wears out and so on, but nevertheless it's there for a purpose – and you've got to take very careful care of it.

WS: And that's, I suppose, where honesty comes in as well with finances and the way you treat your body.

DES: Oh my gracious, Baba's total honesty in relation to it is true, and even down to – the motivation – which he made terribly clear even in the conversations around Meherjee, right at the very beginning of my contacts personally with him.

WS: And I suppose there are so many sanskaras involved with money, always have been, that it's a very important area ... how we relate to the material world is how we relate to money.

Ivy O. Duce and Sufism Reoriented

June 5, 2010

*D*on: So when I arrived in Meherazad, for one of my periodic visits – and this was while Baba was still in the body, but he had given this message to Eruch – "To be sure to tell [Don] the next time I arrived what [Baba] had assured Ivy Duce." And according to Eruch, there were two things that Baba had promised her: the first was that, "From time to time, he would provide an Illumined Master as the head of the Order."

The second promise that he made to Ivy Duce is that he would, "Save her students from any mistakes that she might make."

WS: So Baba said, "Illumined." He didn't say, "God-realized?"

DES: No, according to Eruch. And I was very sure of this, because I always felt that, you know, the ideal was to have a God-realized master who could not make any mistakes, who knew, really knew, the total picture. And so I had never been quite sure in my own mind what "'illumined" actually stood for. Certainly it means that they're pretty high up on the planes, but it certainly is also very obvious that "illumined" is not "God-realised."

The "Order" here refers to the order of Sufism Reoriented created by Meher Baba first with Rabia Martin, and then succeeded by Ivy O. Duce with Don E. Stevens. – LCW

They are two distinctly different terms. I never did really get to the bottom of clarifying just precisely how far "illumined" carried the person. I would be fairly sure that it's through the sixth plane.

WS: My understanding is that it's either fifth or sixth plane; it's one of the words that's used ...

DES: Well, this was my offhand assumption, and I never did check it carefully ...

WS: Don, this meeting you had – with Baba – when he

explained to you what he'd offered Ivy and the Sufis...?

DES: I did not meet with Baba.

WS: It was with Eruch?

DES: He told Eruch to tell me what Baba had promised Ivy. He thought it was that important – not to run a risk that it would get lost and forgotten in the shuffle.

WS: It wasn't Eruch being just a translator ... ?

DES: No, this was a command from Baba himself, to be sure to tell Don about these two important promises he had given Ivy Duce ...

WS: It's very important what you have heard. And can I just clarify, Don, about when Eruch told you about these two things that Baba had promised Ivy? What kind of time period was that?

DES: Oh, well, that was back in the days of Baba being in good health. Baba was functioning well, so it had to be somewhere, I would say, in the late 1950s, because she had two or three personal meetings with him when she travelled.

WS: Right. So it's definitely while Baba was in the body still, and it's not long after Ivy became Murshida then. Was she Murshida in the early 1950s?

DES: Yes, it was not long after Murshida Martin's death.

WS: Yes, and it seems that Baba had wanted to clarify these things?

DES: She had accepted from Murshida Martin the responsibility for being the Murshida. But she had her qualms and doubts about it, and took them up with Baba. When

About illumination, Meher Baba clarified, "A higher state of understanding is permanent illumination, through which the illumined one experiences and sees all things as they are. In this state, one feels in harmony with everyone and everything, and realizes the divinity in every phase of life, and is able to impart happiness to others. Once this state is attained, one attends to all duties and material affairs, and yet feels mentally detached from the world. This is true renunciation." In Lord Meher, p. 1617. Also this, "Ivy Duce felt she did not have the spiritual illumination necessary to work as a true Murshida. Nor did she feel capable or qualified to assume the temporal responsibilities of directing the Sufi Order." ~ Bhau Kalchuri wrote in Lord Meher p. 3183. Lastly, we have reprinted the message "Seven States of Understanding" by Meher Baba at the end of this chapter, which gives Baba's final clarity to this point of illumination vs. God-realization. – LCW

Baba said that he wanted her to assure him that she would carry on, that's when she put his feet to the burner, and said, "I don't know how I can without being ..."

WS: God-realized?

DES: Yes. Now, does ... I just have to ask you as a close trusted friend – how do you feel about my feeling so 100% relieved about Ivy?

WS: It comes across that this has been very important, almost a revelation for you, Don?

DES: It was a revelation: all three of those snaps were revelations.

WS: That they've helped you understand and put in perspective a lot of the history and things you've been through over many decades with close Mandali of Baba.

DES: Yes, this has also been true of just about every single Mandali ... sooner or later, we would have an experience between us where I could not reconcile what they had done with the person that I had come to know, gradually, through Baba.

WS: And the fact that they were known as being close Mandali?

DES: Oh yes, absolutely.

WS: You know people just have this notion of somebody who is so close—physically, emotionally, spiritually to the Avatar, in his inner circle, the Mandali — must be a certain type of person.

DES: Yes, and we assume that it's true, straight through all of their sanskaric complexities — if they are not eliminated, at least they're so close to being eliminated or under control, that it's as if they were perfected already. But then, every once in a while, suddenly you find just an incredible trait, and it can sit around and be there and showing its hint, fairly frequently in fact.

WS: And I think if you look back, at what we know of the Mandali with Jesus and Buddha and other Avatars, they too have very strong, unique characters and personalities and quirks and, you know, things that were there that people might've thought, "Well, what's all that about? That's not quite to my understanding of somebody being spiritual and saintly and things like that." I mean Peter, for example, and how he [denied] Christ three times before the cock crowed, and finally cut off the man's ear who arrested Jesus [in the Garden of Gethsemane] and ...

DES: Well, quite frankly, my third snap, where I connected the Mandali as being the special cases, just explained so many, many, many really tough experiences. And none of them had I ever really, as it were, pieced together in a manner where I could wholeheartedly forgive, and just say that is part of the original corkscrew — the one big thing which caused them to have to be taken on by the Avatar. But boy, they are all magnificent human beings. They've been through Hell and tried every way to solve it ...

WS: And to me that's one of the great beauties of people related to Baba: that they're not of a certain type, they're not what you might expect on the spiritual path ... they are unique.

DES: They're not goody-goodies.

WS: They're not. They've got a great grounding — obviously you have to have being on the spiritual path — but they have got very ... they're all very different, they're individual; they're characters, you know. Everything's there. They represent that individualization that has to be so unique, because that's what they are.

October 7, 2010

DES: I want to be very clear that one of the most wonderful, helpful, kind-hearted, warm-hearted friends I have ever had has been Ivy Duce. She helped me before she became the successor to Murshida Martin in all sorts of ways: establishing friendships, introductions. Really she was the one who laid down the trail which led me to Murshida Martin before I'd ever even heard of her. And then in turn through Murshida Martin to Meher Baba. So I owe her a lot on the spiritual path.

And on one occasion after Baba had confirmed her –
Ivy Duce, as the Mushida of Sufism Reoriented, and Baba

specifically wanted her to be the Murshida – she had raised some questions, some doubts as to her capabilities to do that. Principally that she was not God-realized. And so, when I got to India somewhere in the middle or at the end of these various conversations between Ivy and Meher Baba about her fitness, Eruch said that he had a message for me from Baba, and that Baba had asked Eruch, the next time I arrived in India, to be certain that Eruch repeat to me two reassurances/promises given to Ivy by Baba.

The first of these was in relation to her not being a really illuminated, God-realized master, and how could she be sure that she might not make some spiritual mistakes which would be serious. Particularly, I think she was especially cautious about some of the young people – especially I think there was a small group of quite young girls who had a special class with Murshida – and the first thing that Baba asked Eruch to tell me was that Baba had said, "Ivy, I will save your students from your mistakes."
Well, that was of course a very, very potent spiritual promise, but the exact words of Baba—"I will save your students from your mistakes" – this was gradually transformed within Sufism Reoriented to Baba's having promised her that she would not make spiritual errors. And of course that was not what he had promised. Those were not the words that Baba had Eruch clearly repeat to me.

... The other thing that Eruch had been told by Baba to give me the exact wording, was that in relation to God-[realized] Murshids. Although she was not, Baba had promised her that he would provide, "from time to time an Illuminated Murshid for her Order." Those were the exact words. Now, if I remember, 'illumination' occurs on the sixth plane, but it does not mean I think even necessarily that it is immediately followed by God-realization. I've never been particularly interested in all the niceties of this, but that is my vague, general recollection. But at any rate, certainly the words "from time to time" could not be mistaken.

And so when word came through at times, you know, "Isn't it wonderful that the Sufis will always have a God-realized Murshid?" And I said, "Oh, well that's interesting." ...

WS: And those assurances Baba would have given Ivy?

DES: Direct.

WS: Direct. And then he reiterated them to you through Eruch?

DES: Had Eruch give me the message exactly the way he had told Ivy.

WS: So he had told Ivy shortly before, do you think?

DES: Oh, well he ... Yes, it would've been a short time before, but he wanted me to know almost immediately ...

WS: Well, it comes across, Don, the depth of feeling you have for Ivy after all these years.

DES: One of the deepest human relations I've ever had. And to have it come through so I could say, yes, that really explains what went on. And now, thank God, I am free within myself to love her deeply and without the slightest shadow of feeling maybe she made a deliberate decision she had to change things. So that was wonderful ...

Sooner or later, someone must decide to live with Baba's truth in the matter and take the consequences. I have a feeling that it would clear an unconscious error in the background that needs clearing – because Baba's work with Sufism Reoriented is spot on and wonderful and necessary – but there is that one particular, let's say, screwed up business which I understand now, but which is still not as Baba himself expressed it.

WS: So this is for the record, really?

DES: Yes, this is for the public record. But the public record can now say that I feel wonderful about my deep love and admiration for Ivy Duce.

WS: And people will have to take, as they will in their own

way, what you had been told by Baba, and what is understood …

DES: … was passed down by Murshida Duce. It has to be, in some way, scrubbed clean.

Chapter End Notes:

Because of the confusion created by the use of the term "Illumination" and to distinguish it carefully from the term "God-realization", which two states of consciousness are different according to Meher Baba, we have reprinted Baba's message "Seven States of Understanding" (in *Lord Meher* Vol. 7, p. 2618):

Just as there are seven planes of consciousness — seven spiritual states — so also are there seven states of understanding. It is always seven. The number seven is the divine number.

The seven understandings are:

1. Instinct

2. Intellect

3. Inspiration

4. Intuition

5. Insight

6. Illumination

7. Realization

Instinct governs the animal world;

Intellect, humans;

Inspiration for those humans whose feelings are developed — like poets and artists.

Intuition is for those advanced souls who have conscious visions and understanding true to the point. What you understand by intuition is always true. What you understand by intellect is sometimes true and sometimes not.

Souls on the fourth and fifth plane have Insight; their understanding is direct, without thinking with the mind.

Illumination means seeing God as he is. The understanding is divine.

Realization is understanding oneself as God.

~ Meher Baba

 Meherabad, India

September 29, 1940

The Body and Diet

September 24, 2010

*D*on: When I stop to think about how we take care of the body – should we spend ten, fifteen minutes maybe before we haul off this session?

WS: Take as long as you like, Don, this afternoon.

DES: Well … I've not got an indefinite supply of energy …

WS: I can always come back in the morning.

DES: … I've always got to be careful also about getting my meal prepared at a reasonable time. I go on a fairly tight schedule; I just have to. So this one I'm sure I have spoken about, but I want it to be in the official record. One of the first public meetings that I went to with Baba … we drove in the car to and from the meeting … it was a group in a village not terribly far from Meherabad, and we drove over. Baba hadn't seen this group I think for well over a year, so this visit had been planned for quite some time. And when we got there, of course they were all sitting waiting for him in a hall for the occasion, and it was just so wonderful to see this – great joy – at seeing the Avatar again. It just hung in the air.

And so all went in a normal fashion, Baba's gestures being translated and a few questions going back and forth, but not many. Baba doesn't encourage people to break into things, but if something is important, and a person feels compelled, why – he would allow it. So then finally it's time to call the meeting to an end, and this was the first time I had ever seen this done by Baba: he had all of the men line up, and the boys, in one line, and all the women, and the girls, in another line. And then he went down one by one and embraced each person on both shoulders.

Incidentally, so many people I notice nowadays embrace on one shoulder, and that is not the way Baba did it. It was a good embrace on both shoulders. And I can tell you from having had several years of experience of being embraced by the Avatar, it was a real embrace. Warm, affectionate ... you could feel his ribs, you know. You could feel his arm muscles, you know, there was no part of the body that was spared, considered sacrosanct. It was just a warm – fatherly, brotherly – good bear hug, that's just all there is to it.

WS: And on each shoulder, to balance it maybe?

DES: On each shoulder. And then usually, when he broke the embrace (because some of them would try to keep the embrace longer) and finally then you would see Baba give them a poke in the ribs, which they understood. That was the shorthand method of saying look, this is long enough – and smile when you break away! And so they would look startled, then smile and back away.

So I remember Baba had been, let's say, embracing the men's line ... I don't think he was a third of the way down the line, when he comes across a fellow – I would guess his age somewhere around seventeen, eighteen years of age. I don't know whether he was still in school or not, or whether he worked part-time, but when Baba saw him, Baba didn't go up to him and embrace him. Baba stood back and looked sort of horrified and gesticulated (I think it was Adi Sr. who was the interpreter that evening), and Baba's words were, "And you – what's happened to you? You look really pulled down." You know this is the expression they always use [in India]: "pulled down."

And the fellow looked a little bit startled and said, "Oh, Baba, I was hoping you wouldn't notice it." He said, "I lost my job."

And Baba said, 'How do you eat, if you lost your job?'

He said, "Well, I had to get a [new] job. I was a clerk before, but now I had to get a job, [doing] manual labor, digging ditches and things like that."

And Baba said, "Digging ditches? But that should build up your muscles rather than run you down. Aren't you eating properly?"

And the boy said, "Well, Baba, as you probably know, I'm

terribly anxious to try to make Realization in this lifetime, with your grace and assistance, and so I'm a vegetarian."

Baba looked at him, horrified, and said, "You, a vegetarian? And you're doing manual labour, like that? How do you expect your body to be able to stand it? No wonder you're pulled down."

And the boy said, "Well, Baba, it's more important for me to try to get spiritual Realization with the great, great grace of having you here."

And Baba said, "But if your body can't stand it, and your body decides it's had enough, where's the spiritual Realization going to come from?"

And the boy said, "Well, I just have to trust to luck that it's not going to work that way."

And Baba said, "Look, you simply cannot do that amount of work on a vegetarian diet and Baba wants you to eat meat – good, red meat – at least once a day." And the boy looks horrified …

And this was Baba's advice to a sworn vegetarian who wanted to be a vegetarian for very correct, spiritual reasons. And Baba tells him, "No, your first attention has got to be to keep that body alive, so that there's something to get spiritual Realization, and then next comes diet." He said, "Vegetarian diet is not that important to your spiritual progress." So this story I have to tell, sometime or another, before each new group I come in contact with. And it does not make hits.

WS: {Chuckles} Why ever not!?

DES: So there we are.

HEAD AND HEART

July 10, 2010
{The anniversary of Meher Baba's silence.}

*D*on: I've already discussed more thoroughly this question of honesty and what I'd found its importance to be simply in relation to spiritual truth, the truth that matters, and how it helps enormously to get to the bottom of problems with sanskaric impressions. So then we go on to a very important point involving myself on two occasions when Eruch, Baba, and I were working on editing problems on books that Baba had asked me to take on. Baba just suddenly, for no reason that I could see, stopped the conversation, looked at me very, very quietly, reflectively for a few seconds. And then he would gesticulate to Eruch something or another, which Eruch would then repeat to me.

And this was the second time that he brought up a subject that he treated twice in that manner, but it seemed to have such enormous spiritual importance that the fact that he repeated it twice, told me indelibly, "Don, this is an extremely important point spiritually from Baba. And sooner or later it is going to become garbled, misunderstood, perhaps even convoluted and turned on its head by even Baba's direct followers. And it will be up to you to say, well, [with] that particular point I happen to know how Baba felt about it, because he brought it up twice." And each time it was in a personal context, but it was simply obvious, especially when he did it the second time: that he was referring not to the personal aspect of it for Don Stevens, but as

Meher Baba said, "There is no fundamental opposition between spirit and matter, or if you like, between life and form. The apparent opposition is due to ignorance and wrong thinking. Hence, the remedy lies in the continuous practice of right thinking, in permanent illumination resulting from the balance between head and heart. This is the illumination which I intend to give." In Lord Meher, p. 1626 a key, basic spiritual truth of enormous importance.

At any rate, the first time that he did [speak] on this particular subject, he had been staring at me silently and reflectively ... that means without twitching his fingers even. And he would turn to Eruch, and then Eruch would tell me what Baba had just said to him. And [Eruch] said, "Don, Baba has just said to me, 'Eruch, I think Don has almost the perfect balance between head and heart. What do you think?'"

And because Baba had already done this on a very personal matter, Eruch didn't look flummoxed as he had before. He just immediately looked quite certain of himself. He said, 'Yes, Baba, I agree totally.'

And then several months later, on one of my early next trips to visit Baba (which meant it was at the end of some petroleum business that I had to do, within one-day's flight of Baba), Baba turns to Eruch again, after he's looked very fixedly at me, and says (as if he were saying something brand new, but it was the second time that he had brought it up) —and that was simply, "Eruch, I think Don has an almost perfect balance between head and heart."

And Eruch agreed, I think deliberately and enthusiastically, "... Yes, I agree ..." because Eruch did consider me as being absolutely honest and balanced between head and heart. He made no bones about letting me know. He wouldn't sit and praise me, but in the way things would roll out when we'd be conversing with other Baba followers, it became apparent. Eruch was always letting people know that he had this special conviction about Don's morality and healthy set up. And so he'd simply said, "Yes, Baba, I agree."

[At] the times that Baba brought that up, I didn't feel any particular quarrel in anything that Baba said about the relative value of head and heart. Baba talked a lot about love, but he talked a lot about also taking balanced positions, you know. This was still not at the point when he announced twice in

Mandali Hall (at Meherazad) that his Avataric gift to humanity
would be that of "intuition being generally available to all of
humanity" – and used even in major decisions in regard to things
like engineering, the scientific disciplines, and mathematics. I
would've thought intuition would be great for artists, you know,
creative people – but an engineering problem? How do you get
intuitive about something with all these struts and stresses and so
on, that have got to be measured and worked out mathematically!
So it was a great surprise when each time Baba brought this
up. But he said, however, the immediacy of the answer and the
general trustworthiness of intuitive information should not
lead you to assume that there can be no faults with it, that it is
straight from God ... faultless. You must choose the most readily
available logical-proof method and double-check that intuition
by the most readily available mathematical, or logical, means that
are accessible to you. That is your responsibility. And so it wasn't
long after Baba had done that, but I think that it was probably
still after he dropped the body, that I began to hear people
talking about the obstruction of the mental – the problem of the
mental.

Baba himself had talked about the problem with the mental.
But that was long after I had become aware of the fact that, in
the generation and the evolutionary working out of humanity,
the beginning and more gradual formation anatomically of the
mental body was a very late development. And of course Baba
was very clear that the drop-soul has associated with it a physical,
subtle, and mental body.

WS: From the beginning.

DES: Yeah, right from the beginning. Well, no, not right from
the beginning ... if you take a look at these charts in God Speaks,
there's one where the growth of these bodies is pictorialized. And
Baba is very clear that as soon as the drop-soul emerges from the
Om Point, it is born into a Creation where there's all sorts of
things travelling around in interstellar space. And the drop-soul

just can't avoid having bing-bang-bongs of things passing by and whizzing and bumping into it and so on. And so, let's say, incidences or experiences occur right from the start. And so from that come, let's say, the products of the first iota of consciousness and the first iota of a sanskara.

So that all happens … And then Baba uses a very neat term – I went back and reminded myself — he talks about the drop-soul "associating with" the experience of these things. In other words, they're not flying off into interstellar space. They're right there somewhere or another glued on to it. That was the only thing I could think of, you know, attached like flypaper to the drop-soul. And there ain't even a "body" around to do any housing. And it's because of this sort of scratchy knot of energy wanting to express itself, some way or another, that goads the drop-soul for gathering together an appropriate physical mechanism to let it do whatever it wants to get on with.

WS: Yes.

DES: It's an amazing statement if you bother to go back and reflect on it, how all this happens just so simply and naturally. Just sort of like you've got on a sheepskin coat, and you pass by a field and some thorns that get picked up and start scratching you. And you say, "God damn it, I'm uncomfortable. I've gotta do something!" So you adopt something that will allow this itch to be sidetracked. And so there we are, it turns out to be a physical body adapted to – apt to express – whatever this simple knot of energy wants. So it all goes on very, very interestingly enough and then gradually, as the mental body is formed (Baba is terribly clear), this becomes the storage space. And that was such a relief to me to find that … Instead of just being, sort of hanging around like flypaper, which doesn't strike me as being a very good storage mechanism … There is a body coming along which is adapted to be the storage space.

And so when Baba would talk about the problem of the mental, that to me was the stored sanskaric content. And it sure was an itchy, scratchy sort of a place. And I would think twice about opening the door to that part of the mental body. And so it's a real problem, a mental problem, but it does not mean that therefore mental or logical processes are taboo – far from it. You can get all tangled up and confuse that with reality, and they're associated. But the mental is not the unique, wonderful resource, as some people who are all brains and no heart feel – that everybody else is just a bunch of sentimental nincompoops.

So at any rate, all of that became very clear to me. And I would just get sick at heart frankly, Wayne, listening to highly intelligent Baba people talk knowingly about the obstructions on the path of these mental processes and [about not] getting involved in logic and words, books and things like that. You know, the whole thing ... They just trash! And it becomes instead of, let's say, wise, balanced acceptance—in certain cases doing this or doing that in a logical fashion or so on—just the whole thing goes out ... the baby with the bathwater.

To clarify Meher Baba's position on head and heart we have collected some quotes from Him on this subject at the end of this chapter. – LCW

So I could see then why Baba had brought this up twice with me. And nobody ever likes to hear what I've got to say on this subject, because most people are so convinced that the world has been corrupted by the mental, and all of these formulas and gadgets for doing this and that and the other thing. That we have been corrupted by mental processes and logic, philosophy and books and so on. It is sad to hear rational Baba followers come in and say that, 'The heart is the whole thing. That's got the answer to everything. To hell with the mental.' That is not Baba. It is the balance between the two which is the thing to be achieved. And there's somewhere or another, in ... I think it's in the Discourses in the "The Life of the Spirit" part, where Baba simply says the individual drop-soul cannot return to God before achieving total, complete, perfect balance between the mental and the emotional parts of his nature.

So there we are. People have just got ... I feel myself that in the industrial revolution which became so important in getting people to live decently, without spending all of their time in just trying to get food and lodging together ... to allowlet's say spiritual processes really to take hold and have enough time to reflect, which is necessary. You've got to save time in order to get those things tended to. And it can't be done if the environment is so tough that just subsistence demands all of your time and energy.

So it is terribly important that one gets the physical settled, but it doesn't mean that therefore things associated with it, such as logic and philosophy and so on, are therefore an obstruction. They're not the whole thing, and they can be easily over-represented. And I think that during several hundred years of the so-called industrial revolution—where the produce of science began giving us means of lightening the burden of individual time needed to stay alive, decently alive, so that the spiritual processes had more of a chance to flower—took so much time and effort that actually Dad was at the office unreasonable hours and had very little time to fuss around with the children and be loving. And even mother got so tangled up with gadgets for the kitchen and laundry and so on, that an awful lot of her activity, instead of pouring affection on children, got tangled up with household and budgets and so on. And I do believe that the balance went far over in the direction of the logical, the planned, the rational....

WS: The mechanical, almost.

DES: Yes, right, thanks to the industrial revolution. So kids did get starved ... I remember when I was a kid, many of my kid friends just felt that their parents were admirable people, but just no source of emotional satisfaction to them at all. It was terribly real. And so the Avatar this time had to come in and give great big overdoses of love to start getting the balance set right...

WS: Start getting back again.

DES: ... But then you start getting, let's say, the thing a bit balanced, and everybody becomes so hipped on what they realize what was very important in getting their own lives back on an even keel. They just sort of damn the other side of it. And I think we have gone too far in that direction, quite frankly. Many, many, many, many ... even Baba people. And they ought to know better, because Baba certainly did not say that. This makes me really sad. And I can see why Baba repeated ... That was one of the few things that he ever repeated to me.

WS: To you, on more than one occasion?

DES: Twice. And that was his signal to me that it was really important.

WS: And you think this should go in this volume?

DES: I certainly do, boy. I think this, let's say, is not a moral insult to people. And it doesn't have, let's say, the reputation of some particular person that might be tarnished involved, but it's all of our reputations.

WS: This is something you think needs to be put on record as...?

DES: Yes. And it's gonna be awfully difficult for even a lot of deeply sincere Baba followers to look honestly inside of themselves ...

{Break: Doorbell}

DES: ... so I think that's where we'll stop.

WS: Thank you, Don.

DES: I think we'll have one, maybe two more sessions, and then I think it's time to put it out for a final editing and publish it.

End Notes:

Quotes collected by Laurent from Avatar Meher Baba and His Mandali about the balance of head and heart:

1. "I repeat, materialism and spirituality must go hand in hand. The balance of head and heart must be maintained; the head for discrimination, and the heart for feeling, whereby it is possible to realize infinite consciousness in art, science, nature and in every phase of life."

~ Meher Baba, May 19, 1932 in New York, from a (two page) printed message given to reporters who came on board the ship "Bremen"; See: *Lord Meher (LM)*, p.1616-1618; also see *The Perfect Master* by C. Purdom, p.165-168; Also see *Messages of Meher Baba, East and West*, Adi K. Irani (ed) p. 84-87

2. A question was posed to Meher Baba and this is his answer.

Q: "Do intellectual attainments help or hinder man's progress on the spiritual path?"

Meher Baba: "It is impossible to reach the spiritual Truth and Realization by talks, arguments or by reading books. It can be reached by the heart alone; but that would be a very slow process. But when the heart and the head are equally developed and well-balanced, man's progress is much quicker.

The man in whom the head (intellect) is more developed than the heart, is liable to get idees fixes (fixed ideas), and he becomes attached to his intellectual achievements and superiority. The man with a warm heart has greater faith, and for Love and Truth, he will give up all.

Intellect is the lowest form of understanding, and is developed by reading, listening, reasoning and logic. These processes create an illusion of Real Knowledge.

The higher form of understanding is permanent illumination through which one experiences and sees things as they are. In this state, one feels in harmony with everyone and everything and realizes Divinity in every phase of life and is able to impart happiness to others.

The last and the highest state of understanding results from the merging of the soul into the limitless Ocean of Infinite Knowledge, Bliss and Power. One who has himself attained to this can enable thousands to attain Perfection."

In *The Awakener (Magazine)*, Volume VI, number 3, p. 25.

3. "It is best if there is a balance between the head and the heart, but to combine them and keep them balanced is almost impossible. Even in small, petty matters, the intellect rules the heart and spoils its mood. There is nothing better than if your duty is performed according to my wish, and with a balance between the head and the heart. Try and I will help you. Even as a little salt spoils an entire pail of fresh milk, so also the virtues of a man are nullified by a streak of pride in his character." ~ Meher Baba

Ibid, LM p. 1064

4. There is a long explanation from Eruch in *The Ancient One, A Disciple's Memoirs of Meher Baba*, chapter: "The Future with Meher Baba," p.235.

5. "Hope should be fortified by a courage that can accept failure with equanimity; enthusiasm should be harnessed by the wisdom that knows how to wait for the fruit of action with

patience. Idealistic dreams about the future should be counterbalanced by a sense of the realities of the present. The glow of love should allow itself to be illumined by a free and unhampered play of reason."

~ Meher Baba

In "Meher Baba's Message to Youth"

Ibid, LM p. 2813

6. "Learn the art of taking your stand on the Truth within. When you live in this Truth, the result is the fusion of the mind and the heart and the end of all fears and sorrow."

~ Meher Baba

In *Life At Its Best,* p.p. 23-25 © Sufism Reoriented, Inc.

7. While looking for these Head and Heart quotes I came across writing Don had done on this subject which he gave me in Paris in 2003, on a floppy disk he labeled God Speaks Disk 2, and the file was titled by him simply "HEADHRT" (because of the old limitation on eight character file names with a three character extension). The writing is dated February 22, 2001. We reproduce that writing here for Don's clarity of thought on this subject. - LCW:

Head and Heart

Through the now long years since I was in Baba's presence I have become accustomed to the fact that he had planted when we were together certain key statements which were to come into use in key manners through the years. Even more intriguing was the concurrent realization that often these key statements were obviously of importance not just in one area, but in two or even several. Today, for the first time in some years, I recalled his statement on two occasions when only he, Eruch and I were together, he had suddenly interrupted a conversation on some quite different topic, and commented simply to Eruch, "Don is an almost perfect balance between the head and the heart." As Baba's repeating himself in this manner occurred only on one other subject, I felt it had to be important, but in this case, as in the other, I felt it was given principally to bolster my confidence in myself in order to handle some as yet unknown future situation of crisis.

It was only this morning as I stepped from the shower that suddenly I saw the reason, and its unexpected direction of importance completely stunned me. It had to do with the truing of intuition.

There has never been any lack of knowing that I have a good head, and I have hoped through the years that if the heart were deficient in some manner, then Baba would find the means of raising it to a more desirable level of performance. And there, for better or for worse, I have left that very much under-appreciated comment. But just now, I saw it suddenly in a different context. It was that Baba really meant what he was saying when he emphasized the role that critical reason had to play in the unfolding of God's consciousness of His own divinity. Now I see that Baba's unexpected comment on Don's balance of head and heart relates principally to an important function that reason evidently must play in connection with the gift of intuition as it begins to come into real use as the Avatar's gift to humanity in this incarnation of the Avatar.

The problem is a simple one. Intuition, especially now, is still a fairly fragile commodity, and we have very little stomach for the present to see and take into account the important role of the sanskaras in both blocking as well as in distorting the tender intuition as it emerges.

I have long seen this problem due to the early training both Stewart Edward White and Katherine Ahlstrand gave me in the realm of the coloring that occurs to modify whatever comes through intuitively from the unconscious. I have assumed for many years that one of the principal roles of the companions in a restricted circle of study is its ability to assist with this problem of coloring/distortion of the intuition. My explanation to myself and to others has been that it is statistically improbable that several or all of one's fellow companions will be afflicted with the same strong sanskaras as oneself. In such case the companion is comparatively open to sense as it were or intuit, even better, the problems associated with an intuition of a fellow companion.z

While this is completely logical and I believe is still a valid concept, I suddenly saw this morning that in each individual his own capacity of reason is intended to be available as a truing mechanism for his own intuitions. Undoubtedly this capacity can exercise its truing capability gradually, but is unfortunately completely subject to the strength of the distorting sanskaras which are present. On the other hand, the wisdom qualities of a companion are far more likely to be available and ready to operate in a truing process if their suggestions can be admitted and trusted on the part of the one exposing his intuition. This is especially important because the wisdom of the one intuiting is inevitably clouded by the exhilaration of his intuition. This sense of intoxication is characteristic of the birth of an intuition, and results in a wave of protective sentiment that resists the least implication of fault or weakenss in the exciting insight.

Baba has told us in various contexts of the great value of personal experiences that have passed through the furnace of critical reason. These are not vitiated or false creations of the mental processes, but a resultant which – it is clear from his description – may far surpass the original intuitive content of one's subconscious processes.

Meher Baba's Manifestation

September 25, 2010

*W*ayne: Here we go, Don. It's the twenty fifth of September, 2010 at 228 Hammersmith Grove, and we're carrying on from yesterday ...

DES: Yes, we finished a couple of rather important general subjects. Today I want to go onto another story, extremely important and which very much involves Baba's "Manifestation." Of course, when and how he would manifest has been quite a continuing saga down through the years. Probably the most famous incident was when he told the women Mandali that he was going to choose the occasion of his being in the Hollywood Bowl in Southern California, where he would manifest. A number of the women had gone out and bought some fine new gowns on this final, august occasion they had been looking forward to. Baba had always emphasized the importance of the Avatar's manifestation – giving the whole universe a jolt forward, people becoming aware of his mission. So it has always had quite a bit of aura and importance and mystery after he had, on I think probably two or maybe twenty occasions, predicted something about his manifestation.

WS: Is that the same, Don, as his breaking his silence?

DES: Well, he ventured into his breaking his silence and accident, and even finally he was predicting, as I remember, that soon after he manifested and broke his silence he would die – actually drop the body. So when that started creeping in, people looked forward to it – not with great anticipation – but dread, because that hung over the occasion.

But this has to do with a very curious project. I was taken from my concentration [on my] professional career selling crude-oil in the Eastern hemisphere for Chevron, and brought back to the United States (as I remember it was specifically to become Vice-President of "special projects"). And at any rate, rather unexpectedly I came back … [I] actually spent three years in the home San Francisco office of Chevron.

And so of course I resumed very, very intimate ties with Meher Baba activities, especially in the Bay area. And it was not long into that period when I had a desperate phone call from Ivy Duce (who of course was by that time the new Murshida and was actually living in the Bay area). And we had a very nice quarters for the Sufis on Sutter Street with plenty of room … The first time when we started actually renting quarters, about the only thing we could afford was a little tiny room in one of the office buildings down on Bush Street. So when we got into the Sutter Street office, we could spread out the books, and have nice meetings, and so on. And we really flowered).

And I had a desperate call one day from Ivy Duce, who was at the Sutter Street office: "Don, the strangest thing has happened. There are three hippies

See also the Sufism Reoriented website History page http://www.sufismreoriented.org/history.

who have come knocking at our door!" And she said, "Of course I know about hippies, but I don't think I have ever seen one before. But there are three, and good heavens they are dirty and ragged and bearded. And I just have to be very careful what I say and how I react." She continued, "I'm talking to you privately for a few minutes to ask if you would be willing to talk to these three people, because they're asking questions about Inayat Khan and his relationship [to Murshida Martin], and they are deeply attracted by his poetry. I of course am the proper person to talk to, but because I'm amazed at their appearance, I don't trust myself to do a good job of it. You've probably been around some of these people and will not be as quite disoriented as I am. Would you be willing to make a date with them and talk with them more about particularly Inayat Khan, and Murshida Martin and her relationship to him, which is important?"

So I said – good heavens yes, send them up on Saturday to my home address here (I was out on North Point very close to the Golden Gate bridge) across ... It was a beautiful place with a lovely view and I had a nice apartment there. And I had inherited a canary who was called Fred and who became quite a jewel in the annals of Sufi lore in San Francisco ... I can't go into all of that at present).

So eventually on the Saturday they came. And I must admit when they [rang] the doorbell, and I saw what was actually on my second floor apartment

For more about Don's canary Fred, see his book *Some Results*.

doorstep I said to myself, "My God, I hope the owner of the place – who actually lived there – hasn't seen them coming in. He would probably throw me out!" And so I hastily told them to come in, and they sat down. And I carried on for a few minutes the semi-polite conversation, but I was so fascinated seeing just how unkempt they were, and how little cared for they were, that I couldn't really concentrate too well myself. And I was embarrassed about that.

Until all of a sudden the fellow who had greeted me at the door (and who was obviously the head of the group) put a question to me that was something about the spiritual path and God-realization. And I was so startled, not because it was an intelligent question, but by the sincerity of it. I wasn't expecting this tone of sincerity to come out of this bag of bones and whiskers that was sitting across from me. And I sort of woke up out of my stupor and bemusement with their appearance and thought, "My God, this guy means business, and he is sincere ... This is important."

WS: Do you remember who that was, Don?

DES: I don't. But [at] any rate, he continued on. He was the kingpin of the hippie group. And so coming out of all of this was the fact that we very, very soon saw that what they were interested in was not going to be satisfied by very neatly and polished put questions on a limited basis, but they were actually interested in

– the works. And so I gave myself up and decided I would offer to
them say a "three months course in basic mysticism," which I had
never studied myself, but had done a fair amount of reading by
that time in life. So I thought I could at least organize it around
what I had picked up from Inayat Khan's more organized
teachings. And it was a wonderful group. It began to get out of all
proportion and I limited it to the thirty-five who were present that
evening.

These groups, limited to thirty-five
hippies for three months, went on for
three years and became one of the most
extraordinary, exciting things that ever
happened to me, quite frankly, on the
path. And so I treasured them and on one
of my early visits to Baba … because by

> Don explained in a longer version of
> this story published elsewhere that the
> thirty five people who eventually came
> were not all present from day one. It
> grew to that number gradually in the
> first few weeks. – LCW

that time he had invited me to come and be with him whenever
I was one day jet plane trip [away] from him … and so on one of
these early occasions I told him about this group of hippies. And
he was interested, deeply, at once. And I said to him, "Well Baba,
you know, when I get to mysticism, Sufi mysticism, I've got those
five books Deshmukh put together of the collected … "

WS: Discourses?

DES: " … Discourses, and they take to them like the Bible."

And Baba immediately looked at me beady eyed, and he said,
"Oh, they especially like them?"

And I said, "Yes, Baba. Really, it just seems like a natural
marriage between these hippies and what you have given in these
Discourses."

And he said, "Well now, they aren't very polished, are they?"

And I said, "Well, of course Deshmukh is a highly polished
scholar, and his command of English is tremendous, but still his
styling, especially his sentence structure, is typically Indian. And
I frequently have to go back over a sentence and re-transcribe
the order of a sentence into Western-American or English style

sentence in order to be sure to be understood properly."

And Baba said, "Well, that means that we've got to do something about that." So eventually, of course, he decides that I've got to take on the job of the re-editing them into a new edition. And they actually came out into a little three volume blue-book edition while those hippy groups on basic mysticism were going along, and Baba followed all of that very carefully.

But as I got into it each time revising, re-editing the Deshmukh five volume edition to what became the three volume blue-book edition, Baba kept in very close touch with it. And so on one occasion when I went to visit Baba on one of my periodic visits, he always asked me how it was going. He kept in very close touch,

Now known as the sixth edition of the discourses and just reprinted by Sheriar Foundation: *Discourses* (Revised 6th Edition) by Meher Baba, 4-volume paperback set 904 pp. www. sheriarbooks.org

and he always wanted to know my rate of progress, which was a little bit annoying because of my trying to carry on all of the various pots I had on the stove. It was quite a chore in those days, and this was the first time that Baba, you know, had my feet to the coals constantly on a particular thing, and I felt the pressure of it.

And so finally on one occasion, I had just been editing the Discourses on the subject of meditation and I think, as I remember there were five discourses on meditation, (and I've never been a great person for meditation). I had friends when I as a kid who had Theosophists in the family, and they knew all about meditation and things like this, you know. And they would talk about what their Mas and Pas were doing in their mysticism courses. I would just sort of close off my radio-antenna and not listen at all. So the subject did not appeal to me, but I did tremendously come to what Baba said on sanskaras. And I always – since I read the discourses on sanskaras – considered that was his major contribution to modern mysticism from the Avatar.

So when I found that the discourses devoted to meditation outnumbered the sanskara discourses, I was a little bit hurt and incensed. So when I got to India, I said, "Oh Baba, I've just been editing the discourses on meditation, and do you realize that there are more discourses on meditation than on sanskaras?" Then I looked at my little bag of – diplomacy or non-diplomacy – comments and I said, "Baba, when I stop to think of it, if meditation is that important, how come you've never given me a meditation in all the time we've been together?" And I thought I had Baba over a barrel!

So Baba looked at me very, very solemnly and he said, "Well Don, now we haven't discussed this, but I have to tell you that of the high roads way back, the path back to Realization, to oneness with God, on that path the High Road of all paths is that of love. But the path of love is not always open. When I manifest it is open, and it is fully open. And because it is now fully open – because it is now fully open – it is a relative waste of time to use what is the best secondary road, which is that of meditation." He said, "So if I gave you meditation it would be relatively somewhat of a waste of your time. That's why I've never given you one."

And I certainly realized inside of myself after Baba had finished off that conversation and I was walking out of Mandali Hall door – "My God, Baba has just told me that he has manifested! He is already manifested!" And all this brouhaha about – When I Manifest – is just window dressing. And for some reason or another he had just kept it silent and was using it, obviously, to work on people's sanskaras: getting them to think that he hasn't, and then he's going to, and then he disappoints them, and then he cleans up the mess of their expectancy sanskaras. And so it's one of the most powerful foils that I can see that Baba used to great purpose in that direction.

WS: When do you think he might have manifested then, Don?

DES: Well, it wasn't till, I would say, one or two years later that that same question hit me – well, when did he? And then I remembered that he had always linked several things to his manifestation, and one of the ones that had always fascinated me was that when he manifested he would give all of Creation a great jolt of Avataric energy – a sort of a special prod – and that even the lowliest ant would feel the Avatar's great jolt of Avataric energy.

Meher Baba said, "The Avatar descends from his highest state of divine consciousness to the state of human consciousness. He does not need to pass through the stages of evolution, reincarnation and Realization. He is God always, and comes down directly from his God-state to man-state, and becomes conscious of creation. His benevolent work is universal, and he gives a spiritual push to all objects in creation, inert and living, animate and inanimate both." In *Lord Meher*, p. 2435.

So I began looking around in my mind and I thought – well, gee whiz, I really have become rather conscious of what seems to me like a most unusual "human" which is manifest in young people and all of these hippies. It seems to be that they really started blossoming out in the fifties. I wasn't a specialist in the field, but as best as can remember I began to hear about them at any rate in the fifties when they became important.

And then I thought well, but there is one thing I have certainly been close to and very observant of: I've always had a dog around, and I've had Fred the canary for quite some time, and I inherited for the first time in my life two cats. So I looked at what I can remember about them, and what I remembered when I was a little kid about characteristics of dogs, cats and canaries, and I came to the conclusion that – particularly in the line of dogs I owned – there was a tremendous change. It was almost as if my dogs ... I had never known a more marvelous, regal dog than my Scotch Collie dog – Denny –that my father gave me as my first birthday present. He was a superb, magnificent animal, but I never had the sense that I could almost hear him thinking, and that he knew what I was thinking about, not with little Denny at all.

It seemed to me that when one of my friends who came to live with me to do some schooling for a time and brought a dog – Lucky, a Cocker Spaniel – and Lucky was such an unusually, extraordinary dog because Mani, Baba's sister, had a Cocker Spaniel, so we began exchanging letters on the latest antics of bird-dog Peter and my dog

Lucky and who was "turning into a human being faster." And I
came to the conclusion, my golly, that it was about that time ...
and gee-whiz that went back into the fifties also ...

WS: What late fifties, mid or early or ... ?

DES: Oh well, of course, by the time we really got into that part
it was past the mid-fifties. And it was also around that time that I
inherited the cats from Murshida Martin's old secretary (who died
of cancer up at the Sufi school in Fairfax). So, all of this animal
stuff and various sort of things just snowballed in on me in the
fifties ... so that checked my impression when the hippies started
to appear, and so for myself I triangulated on somewhere in the
fifties.

WS: Right, mid to late fifties?

DES: Yes, mid to late. So this all seemed to make sense to me.
But nevertheless when I came out of Mandali Hall after Baba had,
as it were, spilled the beans to me deliberately that he had already
manifested, I said, "My God, even the Mandali don't know about
this – I've got to tell them." So I went over to the Ladies house,
and there were two or three of my favorites over there, and so I
cornered a couple of them (and I'm not going to say which ones
they were) and said, "Baba's just as good as admitted to me that he's
already fully manifested." They looked at me horrified, horrified.
Just as if I had contradicted sacrosanct knowledge, you know, that I
could say something like that when it was so obvious that Baba was
still saying that he was going to manifest and so and so on would
happen ... he was still pulling that scenario on even them.

So they politely thanked me and said please forgive us,
somewhere or another you must have misunderstood what Baba
said. I saw that their minds were totally closed, and that they were
hurt in addition, that I was their good friend – we loved each other
– it was almost as if I had been unfaithful in this – to them in this.

And so I said then, well maybe if not the Lady Mandali, I'll
try a couple of my favourite male Mandali. So I tried a couple of
them, and I got almost exactly the same ... "Don, you're out of

your mind. This just can't be true. Baba keeps repeating, 'I will do this, and I will do that, it's going to happen so and so and all of the people who are connected with me, even my name will light up like lights on a string," you know, all of that business.

So even the men Mandali – good, hard brass-tacks, down-to-earth-guys that I had selected – would have no part of it.

So I just said to myself, 'Well, this is just absolutely taboo apparently and probably for good reason.' And so, of course, we are still in the period in which one of the most revered authorities for such things is saying something like fifty, sixty years before his calendar says that manifestation is due to come. So all of the Baba community is firmly against ...

WS: ... still waiting ...

DES: ... Yes, that it's going to come along. I know this is going to hit with a terrific thud, a negative bang, but I think it is high time that it ...

WS: ... it goes on record.

DES: ... Yes, that it goes on record ... indelibly. So this is my reason for bringing it out now.

WS: Have you ever met anybody who thinks along your lines, Don, that Baba has [Manifested]?

DES: Well, once in while I tell this story, but I can see that the, let's say, new stream from God still prevails, and so they look sort of pityingly and say, "It's Stevens getting old." So I have never found a person who is familiar with Baba and the Manifestation who would believe the story. So some people I love so much I felt I just had to tell the story to, but it's pretty obvious that this goes into the deck of, "Well now, even Don can make mistakes." So there we are.

WS: Thank you, Don.

The actual quote from Baba about his manifestation: "It will be as when the 'Power House' is switched on; wherever bulbs are connected to it, there will be light. From the bulbs that are of small candle power, the light will be dim; from those who are of high candle power, the light will be bright. If the bulb is fused there will be no light at all. I perform no miracles, but when I break my silence the first and the last miracle will be performed. The time for the 'Power House' to be switched on is so near that the only thing that will count now is Love." In *The Silent Master*, by I. Luck, p. 7.

Bhau Kalchuri

September 25, 2010

*D*on: Now there is one other matter that is also very, very delicate, but I think again this is the time to bring it up officially. That has to do with the so-called "differences of opinion" between Bhau and Don, which is apparently pretty notorious among Baba lovers. Bhau has a deep sense of hurt and indignation about many things that Don does, and cannot resist on various public occasions from criticizing Don for various things that Bhau either believes Don has done, or else chooses to take a negative interpretation. And this actually has its roots in a very important subject, which is why I want to bring it up now in this particular volume …

The actual truth of the matter is that – of all the Mandali living around Baba, the person Baba never put me in harness with on any project happens to be Bhau. And I often wondered why it was that way. And so on one occasion when I was visiting in India and was walking back – I think past the main house where the women were – and was passing by a bench in the garden, there was Bhau sitting on it waiting for somebody, and he deliberately called to me. I had never made any attempt to talk with Bhau, but I had never made any attempt to ignore him either. And he had never made any attempt to chat with me.

For a comprehensive treatment of these subjects, see our book *Mandali Email*, by Don E. Stevens and V.S. Bhau Kalchuri (London: Companion Books, 2005).

But on this occasion he said, "Don, I wanted to tell you something. I know you're tremendously interested in the New Life, in fact I know that Eruch and several of the Lady Mandali have told you their story of the New Life, but I wanted to tell you one thing that came to me directly from Baba, and that was the two or three things Baba said characterized the New Life – that he had

lived through for all time the wandering life, the begging life …
and I think there was a third one? But he said, "Don, Baba had
said very clearly to me … " and he wasn't sure if this was known
" … that certainly the wandering and begging aspects of the New
Life had been lived through completely by Baba with the Mandali,
and will not have to be lived through by the New Humanity in
the New Life." Well that touched me, because I had not heard this
and thought it was a terribly important point, and I felt touched.
So you might say really for the first time I concentrated on my
own inner feelings about Bhau and wondered a bit why Baba had
not put me into harness with Bhau, as it were, on some sort of
important Baba project. And that remained simply a mystery for
some time.

And then Baba dropped the body and we were all getting
older and a number of the things that Baba had asked me to
do in editing and following up, especially on the translation of
things, caused me of course to be involved with books. Then Bhau
became an important member of the Trust, and Mani set up a very
carefully functioning publications committee. And then Bhau,
when Mani passed on, took over that of course, and every once in
a while we would get into a difference of opinion because I would
have to get certain things clear through the Trust, and that meant
that Bhau would have to be involved. So we did begin to have, let's
say, differences of opinion about what should be done.

And I can remember on one occasion when I was so annoyed
… I was on a business trip for Chevron in Western Europe in a
Brussels hotel room. And just suddenly … because I had found
that my manner of keeping in touch with Baba had to be by
having an open conversation with Baba – not as I entertained as
a possibility at one point, of writing letters to one of the Mandali
and asking them to put them in a place in Baba's tomb and it
seemed to work – but this business of having out loud a report
to Baba wherever I was, at least once a day … it seemed to work
beautifully and satisfy me.

So on this occasion I just said to the blank wall of the hotel room, "Baba, what under the sun is going on with Bhau?" And almost immediately I had what I would simply call an intuition, just as if ... and I never try to say to myself this is Baba talking to me. But on two or three occasion the English, the usage of the English was just so typical of what I had gotten used to in conversations where principally Eruch was the interlocutor between Baba and me – Baba's usage of English on two or three occasions – I just said to myself, This is Baba.

But I didn't expect a reply from Baba. I just expected that he would do whatever was necessary when he had asked me to keep in touch with him as a good companion. So on this occasion I just talked to the wall in the hotel and immediately had, let's say, a very, very clear picture, and the part of it that was the most definitive and absolutely clear, brief but no quibbles: "Bhau's great, deep love for Baba."

WS: That's what came through?

DES: Yes, this was simply, let's say, laid flat out – that being the central, controlling thing. Of course no discussion, but I understood that, like human beings still working on sanskaras, he's got problems. But there is no question about the sincerity and the depth of his love.

WS: Underlying everything is this love?

DES: Underlying everything – that is the baseline. And so don't forget that is the important thing: Baba's relationship to Bhau, and Bhau's relationship to Baba. So I sort of did a deep breath and said, "Well, if that's the case, okay, then this is what I've got to accept when I get annoyed with Bhau. That's important, so ... "

WS: To remember that.

DES: ... I will do my best to observe it.

WS: Yes.

DES: And then this was a deep, I trust, intuition and that was such a clear and important one. It was important to me. But still these various different things of getting approval on this and approval on that and difference of opinion on that, you know, it sort of was gradually wearing thin. And then Bhau started having his intestinal blockages and trips to the hospital, you know these things. And on one of the occasions when I was in Poona—when I was checking out of the hotel – I thought to myself, "Oh, God." For I heard among other things that Bhau was in the hospital in a clinic in Poona where he would go when he would have one of these blockages and was recovering. I said, I simply cannot leave Poona, because the hospital is in shooting distance of where I had been staying in the hotel, and I must just go and visit him. So I did.

I went in and, some way or another, I found out he was in such and such a room on such and such a floor. So, unannounced, I just clambered up there and knocked on the door ... went in. He was in a private room – Radha was his nurse, and Radha I knew from donkey's years back – so as I went in, I thought Bhau was in good hands. So I looked around to see where Bhau was. He was sitting cross-legged on the top of his bed and as I looked at him somewhere ... I'm not a person for psychic visions, and I can't say that I saw anything, but what I sensed was just a tremendous, powerful, aura of deep love. And I knew instantly that's what this was: Bhau sitting, meditating on his love for Baba. And I was witnessing Baba's love for Bhau coming back in great big gulps.

WS: Shining through ...

DES: Yes, shining through. It was so moving and so strong ... I've never forgotten it. And so ever after that I've just always said to myself, "Well, certainly there is no doubt about Bhau's sincere, incredible love for Baba and Baba's very deep, reciprocated love to Bhau." And also the manner in which Bhau can give that over to an audience and give them, really, deeply, legitimately, that sense of love for the Avatar. It is a tremendous and real gift. So, that incident was just graven very deeply inside of me.

GLOSSARY

Avatar (adj. Avataric): The total manifestation of God in human form on earth, as the eternal living Perfect Master; the direct descent of Reality into illusion; the Saviour, the Highest of the High, the Ancient One. Also called the God-Man, the Messiah, the Buddha, the Christ, the Rasool, the Saheb-e-Zaman.

Drop-soul: another expression for "the soul," particularly as it is understood in Eastern mysticism where the atma (soul) and Paramatma (Over-soul or Godhead) are considered to be in essence One and the same Reality (i.e. the soul is but a "drop" of God's infinite "Ocean"). Meher Baba said, "Some God-realized persons have, in addition to consciousness of God, an awareness of the existence of other souls who are in bondage. They know all these souls to be forms of the Paramatma who are all destined one day to achieve emancipation and God-realization." (In Discourses, Vol. 3, p. 26, "The Man-God: I")

Gross body (or form): the physical body or form that functions in the gross sphere.

Subtle body (or form): the body of vital energy or pran, which functions in the subtle sphere; the vehicle of desires and vital forces.

Mental body (or form): the causal body, which functions in the mental body; the seat of the mind.

Mandali: a circle of intimate disciples. Sometimes, "Mandali member."

Murshid (male)/*Murshida* (female): Head of a Sufi order.

Mureed: Sufi aspirants.

Om Point: the sound "Om" is the reflection or echo of the Primal Sound, the Word of God, the Brahman Nad from which the whole world has arisen. The Om Point is the most-finite point within the infinity of God's Reality through which the

Creation issues forth.

Planes of consciousness: The states of consciousness experienced by the soul while traversing the spiritual Path. During the first six planes, the soul gradually withdraws the focus of its consciousness from the gross sphere to the subtle sphere and then to the mental sphere: this is involution. At the seventh plane the soul experiences Realisation and knows itself to be God.

Perfect Master: a God-realised soul ... one who retains God-consciousness and Creation-consciousness simultaneously and who works in Creation to help other souls towards the Realisation of God.

Sanskaras (sing. Sanskara; adj. sanskaric): Impressions; accumulated traces or imprints of past experiences, which determine one's desires and (influence) actions.

Sufis: the mystics whose origins lie in the Middle East. Their beginnings are lost in antiquity. According to Meher Baba, their existence began around the time of Zoroaster. Later they were revitalized by Prophet Muhammad (peace be upon him and his family). They exist today in all parts of the world.

Sufism Reoriented: a Western branch of Sufism found in the USA. It was established in 1952 following the handing over to Meher Baba by Murshida Rabia Martin of Hazrat Inayat Khan's "Sufi Order" (which occurred in 1945). It has continued to maintain a vital connection to Baba, whilst maintaining many aspects of a traditional Sufi order. For more information see: Who Brought the Sufis, by Don E. Stevens (2004): http://www.jaibaba.com/mandali/ds/broughtsufis.html

Whim (or *Lahar*): "The cause which led the most finite Nothing, latent in the infinite Everything, to manifest itself as infinite Nothingness, is the original cause called the 'Cause.' This Cause is just nothing but the Whim, or lahar of God. This original Whim can also be called the first 'Word' uttered by God – 'Who Am I?'." – Meher Baba, In *God Speaks*.

ACKNOWLEDGMENTS

From Wayne:

Acknowledgments should be given in the first instance to Kathryn Harris, for all her patient and methodical transcribing of the vast majority of these recordings and the encouragement she gave, especially in the early stages of this project. To Laurent Weichberger for his ready support, advice, and willingness to help edit and format this book. A beautiful job too, my brother, on Don's biography ... "Little Bear," he would have been so pleased. Also Sevn McAuley, my, at times, long-suffering companion of Companion Books, whose technical expertise and business acumen make up constantly for my endless struggles in these areas of modern life. Again, another of those without whom this book would still be a work-in-progress.

And to those fellow editors of Neti-Neti mentioned previously in the Introduction, and to the following directors of the Beads charity, whose feedback at times has also been crucial in the development and unfolding of this book: Marnie Frank; Cynthia and Richard Griffin; Georgina and Robert Hartford; Renate Moritz; David Lee; Deborah Sanchez; and to Jane Hoskin, who I must thank especially for her assistance in the early stages of editing.

Finally, to the memory and spirit of our dear friend and elder brother on the path, Don Eugene Stevens ... you are missed more than any of us can say. Dear Don, without a doubt you touched so many hearts and helped us appreciate how life can and should be lived, more richly and deeply, in the constant presence of our Beloved Meher Baba – the One behind the many – and through the "inner links" that both bind and realize us in His awakening grace.

From Laurent:

Thank you first and foremost to Daniel J. Sanders for your tireless work with Don for Baba (even under duress). Don chose well when he wanted Danny to join the "Carry the Torch" seminar series. You carry it well brother. Your edits on this manuscript were perfect.

My deep gratitude to my brother Wayne Smith, spiritual companion, for allowing me to help with this work, it is my honor to do so.

And finally, of course thanks to My Beautiful Big Bear Don and Mashuq Meher, wherever you both are – for believing in me, loving me, and working with me year after year. Avatar Meher Baba Ki Jai!

www.ingramcontent.com/pod-product-compliance
Lightning Source LLC
Chambersburg PA
CBHW071227090426
42736CB00014B/2997